Archaeology

Polity's *Why It Matters* series

In these short and lively books, world-leading thinkers make the case for the importance of their subjects and aim to inspire a new generation of students.

Helen Beebee & Michael Rush, *Philosophy*
Nick Couldry, *Media*
Robert Eaglestone, *Literature*
Andrew Gamble, *Politics*
Lynn Hunt, *History*
Tim Ingold, *Anthropology*
Katrin Kohl, *Modern Languages*
Neville Morley, *Classics*
Alexander B. Murphy, *Geography*
Geoffrey K. Pullum, *Linguistics*
Michael Schudson, *Journalism*
Ann B. Stahl, *Archaeology*
Graham Ward, *Theology and Religion*
Richard Wiseman, *Psychology*

Ann B. Stahl

———————

Archaeology

Why It Matters

polity

First published in 2023 by Polity Press

Polity Press
65 Bridge Street
Cambridge CB2 1UR, UK

Polity Press
111 River Street
Hoboken, NJ 07030, USA

ISBN-13: 978-1-5095-4986-3
ISBN-13: 978-1-5095-4987-0 (pb)

A catalogue record for this book is available from the British Library.

Library of Congress Control Number: 2022939406

Typeset in 11 on 15pt Sabon
by Cheshire Typesetting Ltd, Cuddington, Cheshire
Printed and bound in the UK by CPI Group (UK) Ltd, Croydon

For further information on Polity, visit our website:
politybooks.com

To the next generation, starting with
Josephine Ann and Abigail Marguerite White.
Know whence you came and learn from the past
to create a brighter future.

Contents

Acknowledgments

Grateful thanks to colleagues who shared images: Akin Ogundiran for the Ilé Ifè figure; Patricia Crown for the White Mountain Redware bowl; and Diana Greenlee for the Poverty Point base map. I am grateful to the National Commission of Monuments and Museums, Nigeria, for permission to include Figure 4. Thanks too to Peter Stahl for serving as a sounding board for ideas and providing helpful input on content. The book benefited from the constructive suggestions of anonymous reviewers of the volume proposal and manuscript, for which I am grateful.

I

Archaeological Perspectives

> Go back to where you started, or as far back as you can, examine all of it, travel your road again and tell the truth about it. Sing or shout or testify or keep it to yourself: but know whence you came.
>
> James Baldwin, *The Price of the Ticket: Collected Non-Fiction, 1948–1985*, (New York: St. Martins, 1985), p. xix

As a girl growing up in an Ohio town on Lake Erie's south shore, I was fascinated by the contents of a dusty cigar box on a shelf in my father's garage workshop. It held stone "arrowheads" of varying size, shape, and color. My father collected some from plowed fields around his boyhood home in southeastern Ohio. His father, a ceramic engineer who spent his working life around clay pits and brick factories in the American Midwest, collected others. Some likely came from his maternal great

1

uncle who moved to New Mexico in the 1880s to stake a claim during a turquoise and silver mining boom. Among these was an ancient Clovis spear point, an iconic stone tool that archaeologists associate with the earliest inhabitants of the American Southwest.

I understood these stone objects as things from the past – relics of "Indians" who lived on lands known to my settler ancestors as Ohio. But as a schoolchild, I knew nothing of the Erie people for whom the nearby Great Lake was named, nor of the ancient Indigenous Americans who built the earthworks and effigy mounds that attracted tourists to Ohio's southern counties. I was unaware that landscapes around me bore traces of generations of Indigenous action, as did the landscapes met by my paternal grandmother's Puritan ancestors when they arrived on the shores of land they called New England.

Though my Puritan ancestors imagined themselves as settling a wild place in need of taming and fencing, they benefited from landscapes and resources created by generations of Indigenous Americans. The cleared areas where Indigenous Algonkian people grew their staple maize, beans, and squash created edge environments that attracted animals like deer. These clearings also suited the cows and pigs that Puritans brought with them on their ships, particularly so because Indigenous gardens were unfenced. So too did Puritans benefit from Indigenous technologies they adopted for living in a world they called "new." The earliest Puritan settlers modeled their houses on Algonkian wigwams and borrowed technologies like snowshoes and canoes, vital to the fur trade that sustained their colonies. Puritan survival also depended on growing "Indian corn," domesticated thousands of years earlier in the neotropics and refined by countless generations of Indigenous farmers. In short, they benefited from infrastructure created and stewarded by Indigenous communities whom the Puritans and later settlers dispossessed and displaced.

This story is not peculiar to America. Wherever we live, the histories of earlier generations lie underfoot and in the landscapes, plants, and animals that surround us. But this is history viewed dimly if at all through the texts that are a historian's primary sources. Deep-time histories of human-modified landscapes, our relations with plants and animals, our technologies for acquiring food, of creating shelters, our ways of living together in societies small and large – these are subjects for which archaeology provides primary evidence and sheds light on whence we came.

Archaeological Perspectives

A simple classroom exercise illustrates why archaeology matters. A wide chalkboard provides an ideal canvas, but a sheet of paper turned on its long side will serve. Draw a line edge to edge to represent the time span of human history. Make a mark at one end to represent 3 million years ago, the point by which we know that early human ancestors in East Africa were making stone tools.[1] A tick at the opposite end represents today. Make a mark representing .5 million years ago (one quarter the line's length from "today"). Between .5 million and today, add a tick representing 100,000 years ago and then one at 50,000. Now divide the line between 50,000 years and today with four ticks, the last representing 10,000 years ago. Halve the line between 10,000 years and today. This last tick marks the time around which early writing systems developed in the Middle East, with early writing in China appearing by somewhat over 3,000 and Mesoamerica about 2,500 years ago. Societies across the globe adopted this innovation, though unevenly and some in recent centuries. The point of this exercise? Important as written sources are, they cover less than 1 percent of human history. If we want to learn about the remaining 99 percent, we must draw on other sources.

One possibility is oral history. All societies relay their history from generation to generation, for example as origin accounts, epics, or odes. Once dismissed as unreliable by scholars, oral accounts convey intergenerational wisdom, including memories of times long past. They provide insight into how past experience influenced a society's values. Oral histories are selective and, in this way, no different from texts. Like texts, they tend to be richer in reference to recent times, but they can be important sources of historical understanding, and particularly so for societies that emphasize oral literacy.[2]

Archaeological evidence also has limitations. Its material sources are biased toward durable (stone, metal, ceramic) technologies over perishable ones (basketry, cloth). Accurate interpretation requires close attention to how objects came to rest in the ground and whether their context was disturbed afterwards. But from the time when our hominin ancestors began to make, use, and discard stone tools, material remains in the form of what archaeologists call *artifacts* (things made or modified), *ecofacts* (resources like plants and animals used or modified by people), *features* (modifications of the earth's surface by digging, mounding, building) and their *associations* (spatial relations or context) provide valuable evidence for understanding past lifeways. By focusing on material remains and their contexts, archaeological methods and techniques extend historical understanding to any time or place in which we find traces of people interacting with things and surrounding landscapes. This applies equally to times "covered" by writing: archaeology lends insight into aspects of life and the lives of people not described in texts. It can also challenge what we learn from written sources. For these reasons and more, archaeology matters.

A young person today is more likely to be introduced to archaeology through a video game than an arrowhead collection, but its lure and fascination remain. Films and gaming portray archaeologists as treasure hunters and tomb raiders in search of powerful relics and ancient secrets. These adventurers succeed while narrowly escaping threats: the undead, hostile natives, or rival archaeologists. For the record, I have never had to outrun a thundering boulder while doing archaeology, nor is a bullwhip part of my tool kit. But real-world archaeology holds a fascination nonetheless, appealing to public curiosity about the past as demonstrated by the success of periodicals like the *National Geographic* or *Archaeology* magazines and a steady flow of documentary films. Though platforms like these only sample the range of what archaeologists do and how they contribute, they attest to a widespread public curiosity about archaeology's subject matter.

On the subject of stereotypes, let's set aside another. Archaeologists do not dig up or study dinosaurs. That is the work of paleontologists. Their timeline requires an even wider classroom chalkboard!

So how can we characterize archaeology? In keeping with popular imagery, it can be exciting, if in a more garden-variety way than depicted in *Raiders of the Lost Ark* or *Lara Croft: Tomb Raider*. Whether digging in a garden, walking a plowed field, or participating in a research excavation, there is wonder in finding old things. Being the first to see or handle an object untouched for centuries or millennia can be thrilling. Perhaps you have had the privilege of visiting one of many iconic sites around the world: Stonehenge in England, Egypt's Giza Pyramids, Chichén Itzá in Mexico, Machu Picchu in Peru, Cambodia's Angkor Wat, southern Africa's Great Zimbabwe, or the terracotta army of Emperor Qin Shi Huang in China, among many others. If so, you know first hand the frisson of being among awe-inspiring monuments and the handwork of ancient people. Walking the streets of Pompeii, made accessible through the work of generations of archaeologists (Figure 1), we marvel at the scale

Figure 1. Mt. Vesuvius looms over one of many paved streets in Pompeii lined with brick edifices of ancient Roman buildings that are open to tourists. The baker Terentius Neo and his wife, pictured on the front cover of this book, might have walked these streets on a daily basis. Photo by the author.

and preservation of the ancient Roman city. We feel goosebumps under the gaze of baker Terentius Neo and his wife, captured in a fresco found in their Pompeii workshop home and reproduced on this book's cover.

Archaeologists are puzzle solvers, though not of the kind that unlock ancient tombs. Our puzzles involve piecing together clues from finds and their contexts to lend insight into past lifeways. Anyone who has paused to watch an excavation in progress will know that the work is time-consuming, painstaking, and more often tedious than exciting. Even more so the lab work that follows as archaeologists count, weigh, measure, and otherwise describe and analyze excavated materials.

Our puzzle solving is akin to assembling a jigsaw puzzle without the aid of the finished picture. This is particularly so for archaeologists working in regions with little prior research or in contexts where other sources (written, oral) are unavailable. Where we dig – in a temple, a palace, a humble household, or a garbage heap – and how much we dig determines which puzzle pieces we have to reconstruct the wider "picture." We never have all the pieces. We work with samples, from which we make wider inferences and claims. The quality and number of our samples have implications for the reliability of our insights about a region or period, which is one of the reasons why ongoing research can spark vigorous debate and change what we know about the past.

If you are a jigsaw enthusiast, you know how joining the wrong pieces stymies your progress. Our views of the big picture often run in advance of the puzzle pieces, creating hunches or hypotheses about what to look for among remaining or future ones. Sometimes these hunches are wrong. Being open to clues lent by new pieces helps us to reform interpretations and understandings. As we will see, archaeological evidence can reveal startling insights that force us to reconsider what we think we know about the past, so long as we remain open to considering its surprising implications.

Our puzzles vary in scale and resolution. Some archaeologists spend their careers puzzling over a single artifact type, site, or region. Others puzzle at wider scales – focused on longer units of time or wider landscapes. The pace of archaeological research has accelerated over recent decades to the point that keeping up with current research outside one's specialist area is daunting. For this reason, among others, global and popular syntheses of archaeology often lag behind the current state of research and perpetuate outdated understandings of human history, a point to which we return in pages to come.

Because it requires many human resources, archaeology is expensive and often depends on government research or non-profit funding. Volunteers or students-in-training who pay to participate are the lifeline of many archaeology projects. In countries where governments struggle to provide basic services to their citizens (in other words, much of the world), the cost of research means that archaeological projects are often funded by foreign agencies and staffed by archaeologists from elsewhere. The same can be said for archaeology in the settler states that encompass all of the Americas, portions of the Pacific, and some African regions. Here the history underfoot is that of people dispossessed and displaced from their ancestral homes and marginalized within those states, few of whom have sought careers in archaeology until recently.

In this and other respects, archaeology is colonial. While societies the world over and through time have demonstrated interest in ruins and old things, archaeology's disciplinary history is intertwined with imperial expansion and colonialism. Early studies and collecting of ancient Egyptian antiquities took place during Napoleon's 1798–99 Egyptian campaign and those materials remain in

Europe's museums today. The founding of formal colonies enabled access to foreign sites, with early excavations often motivated by the aim of filling museums at home. Excavations in foreign lands long served as training grounds for foreign students, with little opportunity or training available to locals. As historian of archaeology Bruce Trigger observed,[3] archaeologists who came from elsewhere were little motivated to celebrate the achievements or challenge negative characterizations of colonized peoples. Although critiques mounted by Indigenous and colonized peoples over the last half century have led to substantive changes in how archaeology is practiced, colonialism remains embedded in archaeology as it does in other disciplines, even if their practitioners less often acknowledge it.

In some places, the history we study or learn about through archaeology is "ours," implying a "we" from whom we are descended. "We" and "ours" are telescoping terms. They encompass broadly or narrowly: we humans, we Europeans, we Britons, we from a specific place. Their scope is more often implied than stated and, as the scope narrows, they imply exclusions: a "them" and "theirs," which often goes hand-in-hand with perceived difference. The more ancient the remains, the more such ancestral connections become muted, perhaps blurred by ancient migrations. For those of us living in settler states whose ancestors came from elsewhere, much of the history underfoot is of other people dispossessed and historically marginalized. How we claim these pasts or the right to study and tell their stories is consequential in the present, which is why archaeology is also political.[4]

In short, how we do archaeology matters. A patchwork of regulations today guides the practice of archaeology in different areas of the world. Much archaeology in the global north is funded through mandated Cultural Resource Management (CRM) processes. Some countries have national antiquities laws that regulate excavations, govern the export of archaeological material, and set standards for reporting. In other countries, laws govern federal- or state-owned lands but leave work on private lands unregulated. But for too long archaeologists paid little attention to the interests of local communities in their proposed projects. This is a particular problem in colonized regions of the world, where archaeologists seldom consulted descendant communities. Communities therefore had little say in the questions asked, the sites dug, or the fate of materials once excavated. These practices created animosity between them and archaeologists, particularly pronounced in the United States, which led

Indigenous people and other advocates to press for passage of the Native American Graves Protection and Repatriation Act (NAGPRA), enacted as Federal law in 1990. Although some archaeologists resisted the return of ancestors and cultural property mandated by NAGPRA, the law led to new forms of collaboration between archaeologists and Indigenous communities. For this and other reasons, archaeologists today see collaboration with communities as increasingly vital to their research.[5]

While archaeology can result in preservation of fragile things, archaeological excavation destroys its primary resource: things in context. Studying things in context differentiates archaeologists from collectors, antiquarians, and looters. Antiquarians and collectors share with archaeologists an interest in old things – antiquities – but their focus is typically on the thing itself, its age, and often its market value. Looters dig up antiquities to supply a market through intermediaries, moving objects from their context in the ground to the lit shelves of well-appointed homes or museums. Things taken out of context lack associations: with other artifacts, with the strata where they were unearthed, and with the wider surrounds in which they were used, had meaning, and were discarded or lost. Associations provide important insight into the age, uses, and meanings of things, among other possibilities. Once removed from the ground, associations are lost, which accounts for why archaeologists spend so much of their fieldwork time measuring, writing notes, taking photos, and bagging and tagging finds according to their "provenience" (find location). These details are key to archaeological interpretation, which is why it is vitally important that we curate and archive field records alongside artifacts to allow for future reinterpretations of sites.[6]

Archaeology is diverse in its aims, topics, questions, and methods. Its wide remit accounts for the many professional contexts in which archaeologists work, from CRM firms to university departments, including stand-alone departments of Archaeology and Prehistory, common in the United Kingdom and Europe, those of Anthropology in the Americas, and Area Studies (African, Near Eastern, Asian) and History departments, together with Classics and Biblical Studies departments, around the world. Depending on the time period and area of the world in which we work, individual archaeologists may think of their work as more aligned to the sciences or the humanities, but our subject matter, methods, and approaches are fundamentally enriched by methods ranging from epigraphy and visual studies to chemical analyses and remote sensing.

Archaeology thus accommodates and is enriched by the sensibilities and insights of wide-ranging approaches and academic backgrounds. In short, archaeology is a quintessentially interdisciplinary subject that benefits from systematic application of scientific method and interpretive sensibilities.

Archaeologists are curious, with each generation posing new questions and seeking new and more insightful means of answering them. Archaeologists engage in systematic inquiry based in evidence derived by studying material remains. Like other arenas of life, doing archaeology is changed by new technologies and advances in scientific techniques. Many were developed for other purposes and only later applied to archaeological problem solving. For example, radiocarbon dating revolutionized our ability to estimate the age of sites after World War II. Based on measuring radioactive carbon decay in organic materials like wood and seeds, the dating technique derived from work of the Manhattan Project that developed the atomic bomb. Where once our age estimations depended on methods like cross-dating with textual sources or relative placement in a stratigraphic sequence (deeper deposits being older than those overlying them, if undisturbed), radiocarbon and other radiometric dating techniques enabled archaeologists to estimate the age of finds more precisely. As an example, in the 1960s archaeologists guessed that early human ancestors occupied East Africa's Rift Valley a million years ago, but radiometric dating now shows that early stone-tool-making ancestors lived there from as early as 3.3 million years ago.

Innovations in radar and laser technologies have transformed our ability to locate and map archaeological sites and wider landscapes. Developed for purposes like tracking and guiding aircraft or remote surveillance of Cold War enemy installations, applications like ground-penetrating radar (GPR) and satellite imagery are used today by archaeologists to locate and learn about sites without – or prior to – digging. GPR uses radio waves to produce high-resolution images of sub-surface features (like walls, floors, and graves), enabling archaeologists to locate and map features in urban areas where digging may not be possible. One newsworthy find was the grave of Plantagenet King Richard III beneath a car park in Leicester, England. Historians knew that the king, who was killed in a 1485 battle that ended the Wars of the Roses, was buried in a friary and that Grey Friar's church was demolished a half century later. Stories had it that the king's body was later dug up and tossed into a river. The approximate location of the church was known, but in the

21st century, it lay buried beneath the pavement of car parks, a playground, and a tangle of utility lines. A 2011 GPR survey located the king's grave in the church choir and later excavation revealed details of a hasty and shallow burial, adding nuance to the events that shaped the transition of power to the Tudor line of monarchs.[7]

Archaeologists also use GPR to locate and study culturally sensitive sites. Working collaboratively with Indigenous communities, they are using this technology to locate the unmarked graves of children buried at Indian residential schools in Canada. These contentious schools lie at the center of Truth and Reconciliation processes in the country, aimed at addressing the harm created by the forced separation of Indigenous children from their families between the 1880s and 1990s, some of whom never returned home. The evidence generated by noninvasive GPR will play a major role in Truth and Reconciliation processes at the forefront of national politics in Canada today and in upcoming years. Here, archaeology matters by supplying evidence relevant to a process of national reckoning.[8]

Other remote sensing techniques have opened new frontiers of knowledge by revealing features that are difficult to see on the ground and locating sites obscured by dense forest or inundated by coastal waters. Aerial LiDAR (Light Detection and Ranging) is a laser mapping technology used to produce high-resolution 3-D digital maps of ground surfaces from the air, enabling archaeologists to visualize landscapes and sites in ways not previously possible. LiDAR flyovers of Stonehenge and surrounds have revealed new earthworks and other landscape modifications that are proving vital to the management of this World Heritage site.[9] Because the technology makes it possible to map ground surfaces below vegetation, LiDAR mapping is especially useful in forested tropical and subtropical places like Mesoamerica and Southeast Asia. For example, airborne laser scanning is revolutionizing understanding of Cambodia's iconic Angkor civilization (9th–15th centuries CE). Long known for its spectacular stone temples, laser mapping has revealed details of wider landscapes obscured beneath the thick forest canopy. Extensive settlements built of less durable materials (earth, wood, and thatch) cover an area of about 400 km^2 in an intensively modified landscape. Khmer people built mounds to raise settlements above floodwaters, and constructed large-scale water management systems (basins, reservoirs, canals) together with roads that connected settlements, temples, and other sites.[10] In short, the scans revealed an elaborate infrastructure in a previously unknown urban landscape. Confirming features identified from the air through ground-truthing remains important, but these mapping technologies enable both new discoveries and ongoing monitoring of known sites subject to looting and heritage destruction, including iconic Angkor Wat.

In common with other fields, the questions asked by archaeologists involve a tension between studying what is widely shared and what is specific to a particular place or time. As such, archaeologists work to shed light on a history common to humanity and address topics about which the public is curious: our origins, how we came to be everywhere, and how past communities responded to universal challenges like climate change. But we also study what is distinctive and different about the histories of people living in different regions and across continents. The methods through which we study commonalities and differences matter, of which more in Chapter 2. However, as a rapid example, consider cities and states, today ubiquitous around the globe – a universal, taken-for-granted feature of modern life. But how did they come to be? Were they everywhere the same? Are there lessons learned from the study of ancient cities and states that apply to cities and states of today and tomorrow?

Early 20th-century studies of ancient urbanism and states asked questions about origins and "firsts." When and where did people first live in cities and become ruled by states? What characteristics did so-called "archaic" states share? Historians, philosophers, and political scientists all posed these questions, but written sources alone could not answer them. Archaeological evidence was critical to understanding similarities and differences. Like colleagues in other disciplines, early archaeologists were most interested in what ancient cities and states allegedly had in common: monumental architecture; systems of writing; rigid hierarchies of elites and commoners headed by despotic rulers; specialization among workers; the wheel; irrigation agriculture; among other characteristics. Guided by this checklist approach, early scholars were blind to the varied forms of ancient urbanism and states in different areas of the world, which decades of painstaking archaeological research across the globe has since revealed. Archaeological investigations make clear that urban life did not depend on the invention of writing or wheeled conveyances. Nor did people living in cities and states share the same social systems or modes of economic and political organization.

Despite variation, archaeology also provides evidence for similarities in how urban elites sought to further and maintain power in the face of non-elite resistance and how they responded to competition from neighbouring states. It helps us to see commonalities in how leaders of ancient states exercised power through everyday activities and special occasions alike, while also showing how common people cooperated with or contested state power. Archaeology has helped us to appreciate the social diversity within ancient cities, the result of people coming from surrounding areas, bringing with them their distinctive ways of living and worshiping while developing new ways of living together in large-scale settlements. Whereas earlier understandings stressed the unmitigated power of kings and the endurance of states, we know more today through archaeology about the mix of hierarchies (e.g., social, religious, economic), modes of control, and fragilities of ancient states,[11] all of which potentially hold insights for the future, about which more in Chapter 5. A key take-away from the study of ancient states is that they are often precarious, their collapse often gives rise to novel arrangements, and social systems in the hinterlands of state centers often persist after central authority dissolves. Moreover, evidence shows that what earlier scholars characterized as catastrophic, apocalyptic collapse (e.g., of ancient Mayan or Khmer civilizations) is frequently exaggerated and was differentially felt, with local circumstances conditioning how commoners and elites alike experienced the dissolution of long-lived cities or states.

In short, archaeology matters because archaeologists ask questions of the past that are pertinent today and to the future. It offers longitudinal, long-term perspectives as well as fine-grained ones centered on daily life. By entering the past through a study of things and wider landscapes, archaeology enriches our understanding of history and the world in which we live today, its evidence often revealing surprises – telling us things that run counter to conventional wisdom. It also helps us to appreciate how present-day arrangements – whether in the layout of cities, the forms of connection between world regions, or the configuration of landscapes around us – carry forward imprints of the past. Fundamentally, archaeology matters because it offers perspectives and evidence that expand our understanding of the world around us and help to enlarge perspectives on the future.

A linear path did not lead from my fascination with the cigar-box arrowhead collection to becoming an archaeologist. Other childhood incidents piqued my interest in things past, including the monthly arrival of *National Geographic* magazine, rich with images of ancient wonders. A book on Greek mythology checked out from the public library led to my fleeting determination to become a mythologist, an aspiration quashed by my 4th-grade teacher, who told me that this was not a job. She suggested instead that I might want to become an archaeologist. After learning that this required four years of university beyond high school and another four years of school after that, I set my sights on becoming a truck (lorry) driver. In the end, I enrolled in university as a retailing/marketing major, but, through the advantage of a general liberal arts education, rediscovered archaeology as a subject matter within anthropology. My middle-class parents were puzzled by my resolve to study archaeology but, as the youngest of four children and they perhaps weary of the process, I had their blessing to pursue what many parents of the time and still today perceive as an "impractical" profession. I had the good fortune to pursue master's and doctoral studies in anthropological archaeology followed by a university teaching career spent in three countries on two continents. As a student I worked on projects in the US Great Lakes region, the Canadian Rockies, the central Mississippi Valley, Ghana, and Gambia, and, from the early 1980s until now, I have been privileged to work in the same set of communities in Ghana, studying how village life in this rural area has been affected by changing global relations over the last 1,000 years.

I write this reflection on the value of archaeology from Vancouver Island's southern shore, today part of the Canadian province of British Columbia. The history underfoot and in the landscapes around me is that of ləkʷəŋən peoples – present today in the Songhees, Esquimalt, and W̱SÁNEĆ First Nations – whose deep historical relationships to the land are ongoing. Living and working here since 2008 has given me a new perspective on the context and value of archaeology, as has working among communities of the Banda area in Ghana since 1982. These experiences shape my perspective on why archaeology matters. A short book like this is necessarily selective in its examples, but I hope that my reflections on why archaeology matters motivate you to learn more about the history underfoot where you live and to appreciate the value archaeology contributes to understanding our simultaneously shared, distinctive, and entangled histories.

In chapters that follow, my aim is to show how archaeologists "think from things"[12] to enrich historical understanding of times recent and ancient. In doing so, I dip into archaeology's history to describe some approaches that no longer hold professional sway but that continue to influence public imagination. At the same time, I provide examples of recent approaches and research results that lend new insights and demonstrate why and how archaeology matters to our understanding of the past, present, and future.

By way of a quick roadmap, Chapter 2 ("Time and Knowing") looks at how we use knowledge of the world around us to reconstruct times past. A short dive into the history of prehistoric archaeology helps us to consider how European ideas about non-European societies shaped early archaeology and how work over the last half century has been enriched both by new evidence and by new perspectives on time and knowing. In Chapter 3 ("Connections through Things"), we look at debates about the role of so-called "material culture" in shaping our experience of the world – tracing a shift from treating it as the imprint of ideas on the world to considering its active role in making social life and creating connections across societies. In Chapter 4 ("Practice and Knowledge"), we consider different meanings of "culture" and explore how understanding of life in the past and present is enriched when we approach culture not as a durable "thing" but instead as a process involving everyday actions and repeated practices. I show through examples how archaeologists study culture-making processes and tease out practices of knowledge transmission across generations. Finally, Chapter 5 ("Possibilities") takes up the question of how archaeology lends important perspective to our understanding of the present and future, making the argument that archaeology expands our imagining of possibilities as we confront common challenges.

So come, let's begin to think through things together as a way to know from whence we came.

2

Time and Knowing

The past is a foreign country: they do things differently there.

L.P. Hartley, *The Go-Between* (London: Penguin, 1997), p. 5

Traces of past lives are all around us. While cultivating a garden or walking the furrows of a plowed field, we find human-modified things (artifacts) that aided the lives of people in the past: sherds from broken pots, modified stones, metal fragments, charred seeds, and bone fragments. How old are these things, and how were they used? What do they tell us about the lifeways of those who made, used, and eventually discarded or lost them?

Answers come in part from studying archaeological materials, but archaeologists also rely on knowledge of the world around them to develop hypotheses and interpretations about the past. In this chapter, we look at how archaeologists develop understandings of past lifeways using clues from ancient remains, but also by drawing on their knowledge of recent times. In the process, we consider the relationship between time and knowing, an important topic because archaeological evidence is a primary source for understanding most of human history.

Begin by imagining yourself a peasant farmer in medieval Europe. (Need help? Think of *Monty Python and the Holy Grail* as Dennis the peasant [Michael Palin] digs, muddied, alongside his mother [Terry Jones] while providing a lesson on representational government to [Graham Chapman's] King Arthur. If you haven't seen it, it's worth a view!) For generations, you and your fathers and mothers before you have used iron tools to till the soil or hew and shape wood into useful things. As you work the soil before planting spring crops ("Dennis, there's some lovely filth down here," says his mother), your iron hoe hits something hard. Pulling it from the soil and turning it in your hand, you notice its smooth surface, distinct sheen, and sides tapered to a thin edge, but its form falls outside the range of human-made things familiar to you.

Because you have no reference for it, you deem it a natural thing. Like your counterparts elsewhere, you understand it as something created by lightning – a natural (meteorological) phenomenon. In the English vernacular, you call it a thunderstone or thunderbolt; in German, a *Donnerstein*; in French, a *pierre de foudre*; or, if you were among Akan speakers in West Africa, a *Nyame akuma* (god's axe). Literate Europeans called these *ceraunia* (Latin for thunderbolt). Collected as curiosities and valued as amulets to ward off lightning strikes, *ceraunia* were often included in cabinets of curiosities (German *Wunderkammer*), the precursors to modern museums.

Today, we recognize these things as artifacts, commonly called celts. Formed by grinding and polishing stone into shapes with durable sharp edges, celts are a marker of the so-called Neolithic (New Stone Age). Depending on how they were attached (hafted) to a handle (Figure 2), ground stone tools like these were used as hoes, axes, or adzes. Given their utility for clearing woodland and working soil, it is unsurprising that they are associated with times when people began farming, more than 10,000 years ago in some areas of the world. In later millennia, metals – particularly iron – supplanted stone as the primary raw material for making tools in many regions. As a result, polished stone tools and the techniques for making them dropped from

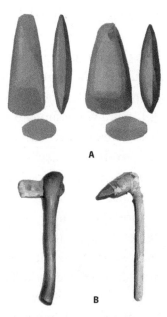

Figure 2. Neolithic polished stone tools. A: Two polished stone celt heads (plan, profile, and cross-section views), about 10 cm in length. B: Celt hafted as an axe (left) and as an adze (right).

iron-using people's repertoires. Thus, during medieval times in Europe and West Africa, people had no direct reference for recognizing thunderstones as human-made tools. However, recognizing them as such was a critical point in perceiving a deep-time past during which people relied on stone technologies.

Thinking through Analogy

Analogy is a logical process by which we come to know the unfamiliar through the familiar. Experiencing something new, we scan our memory for something like it. We assimilate new things to what we know. For example, 16th-century Mayan people referred to horses newly introduced by conquistadors as Castilian tapirs – for the Maya, their closest familiar animal referent. Observed similarities of form may imply other similarities, for example of behavior (in the case of animals) or function (in the case of tools). In short, analogy is the process through which we assimilate new things or experiences to what we know. In the process, we extend characteristics of familiar to unfamiliar things. Ongoing experience may lead us to modify these expectations when we discover that, just because things are alike in some respects, they are not necessarily alike in all respects. As the Maya discovered, horses differ in important ways from tapirs. Ongoing comparison is implied, therefore, in how we come to know through analogy.

Returning to so-called thunderstones, only after observing Indigenous Americans using similar objects did Europeans recognize *ceraunia* as human-made tools.[1] Michele Mercati (1541–93)

32

was among the first for whom the penny dropped. A superintendent of the pope's botanical garden, Mercati had access to the Vatican's vast collection of "curiosities," among which were ground stone axes, adzes, and hoes brought back to Europe from the Americas by 15th- and 16th-century travelers. He noted the similarity of form between "*ceraunia cuneate*" (wedge-shaped thunderbolts) found across Europe and tools used by Indigenous Americans. His analogical interpretation was aided by descriptions of how Indigenous Americans used these tools. In his posthumously published *Metallotheca* (1717), Mercati ventured the opinion that *ceraunia* were tools and that, like the Indigenous Americans of his time, ancient Europeans relied on stone tools. A century later, British antiquarian William Dugdale (1605–86) and his son-in-law Robert Plot (1640–96), Keeper of Oxford's Ashmolean Museum, came to a similar conclusion, with Plot arguing that details seen on American examples showed how ancient Britons hafted theirs. The implication was that you could infer form and function of the complete (hafted) tool from the similarity of its durable component (the celt).

The analogical insight that thunderstones were in fact tools was the "thunderbolt" that established that Europeans had experienced what Danish antiquarian Christian Thomsen (1788–1865) characterized as three technological ages: a Stone Age followed by Bronze and Iron Ages. When coupled with developments in geology and biology, finds of stone tools together with extinct animals laid the foundation for recognizing the Stone Age's great antiquity and establishing the subject matter of so-called prehistoric archaeology.

Artifacts are core data for archaeologists, but they have long aspired to go beyond studying objects to reconstruct the ancient lifeways of people who used them. In his 1865 book *Pre-Historic Times, as Illustrated by Ancient Remains, and the Manners and Customs of Modern Savages*, British banker, parliamentarian and antiquarian Sir John Lubbock (1834–1913) – the man to whom Britons are indebted for bank holidays – built upon Christian Thomsen's Three Age System. Here he introduced the terms Paleolithic (Old Stone Age), referring to times when stone tools were made by chipping or knapping, and Neolithic, marked by the addition of grinding and polishing as stone-shaping techniques. However, the book was equally influential in its aim to reconstruct the "manners and customs" of "pre-historic times." Its title telegraphs Lubbock's method for doing so, which was to flesh out archaeology's fragmentary evidence with descriptions of people who Europeans believed still lived as Stone Age people had. To this end, he devoted more than a quarter of his book to so-called "modern savages," "non-metallic" people from around the world, whom he presented as living fossils who illustrated how ancient Europeans lived.

Digging deeper, we can see how concepts of time influenced ways of knowing in this foundational period for archaeology. Again, Lubbock's title contains important clues to a logic and method that became part and parcel of so-called prehistoric archaeology and prevailed well into the 20th century. Put simply, the logic built on the idea that, despite being contemporary with one another, societies can occupy different temporal spaces. Think here about paired terms like preliterate/literate, prehistoric/historic, traditional/modern, or underdeveloped/developed. Though at first glance these terms do not refer to time, anthropologist Johannes Fabian pointed out that they imply temporal logic and directional movement.[2] He calls these terms of "typological time," in that they imply relative position (an earlier and later form) and directional movement (from one type to another). We imagine preliterate traditional societies as being apart from and before literate modern ones, regardless of whether they exist in the same physical time.

This has implications for how we understand connections among societies perceived as belonging to different stages (of technology, progress, complexity). Despite ongoing interactions, some are perceived as stuck in the past.

By the time Lubbock published his book, the practice of classifying societies into hierarchical stages of so-called savagery, barbarism, or civilization was well established in Europe, and these, too, operated as categories of typological time. These categories have deep histories in western thought, and their meanings took new form during the so-called Age of Discovery (15th–18th centuries) as Europeans colonized other parts of the globe and encountered people who lived differently than they did. Societies were slotted into this hierarchical typology[3] based on technology (stone using vs. metal using), subsistence and economy (hunting-gathering vs. agriculture; specialization and trade), scale of settlement and governance, among other characteristics. Conceived as a progressive scheme through which all societies move (from savagery to barbarism to civilization), these categories provided the scaffolding for 19th-century social evolutionary perspectives that informed so-called prehistoric archaeology at its foundations. The colonial implications are self-evident: societies thought to be on the scheme's lower rungs were deemed "primitive," yet-to-progress, and in need of civilized oversight.

Returning to the use of the role of analogy in archaeological interpretation, these categories of typological time guided how early prehistorians selected societies to "illustrate" the past. Lubbock used descriptions of stone-tool-using "modern savages" (Hottentots, Indigenous Australians, and Native Americans) to supplement fragmentary evidence from Paleolithic and Neolithic times in Europe. As Johannes Fabian pointed out, and as illustrated in Figure 3, this logic implied that traveling in space (the x-axis) is like traveling back through time (y-axis).

Archaeology and other disciplines dropped the denigrating terminology of savagery and barbarism from their vocabulary during the 20th century, but new classification schemes carried forward the assumption of a ladder-like hierarchy, with temporal implications. By the second half of the 20th century, archaeologists classified the kinds of societies they studied in terms of subsistence and economy (hunting-gathering, agricultural, or those involved in surplus exchange), perceived levels of complexity (tribes, chiefdoms, or states), and scale of settlement (village, town, or city), among other variables. Despite using different terms, each set

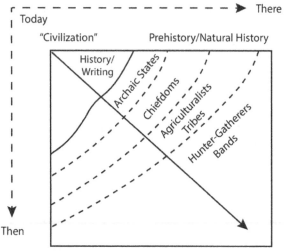

Figure 3. Schematic representation of traveling in space (here to there) as a way to imagine the past (today to then). The invention of writing separates "history" from "prehistory." After Fabian, *Time and the Other*, p. 27 (see note 2 this chapter).

implies temporal relations (earlier and later forms) and directional movement.

These classification schemes have long provided the narrative scaffolding for popular texts on world prehistory. Early chapters focus on the origins of early human ancestors in Africa and follow their migration out of Africa to the farthest reaches of the globe. Chapters on mobile Paleolithic hunter-gatherers commonly draw insight into those times from living peoples who hunt and gather as a primary way of acquiring food. Later chapters discuss Neolithic first farmers, moving on to Bronze Age craft specialists and ultimately Iron Age states. With each topic, the spotlight directs the reader's attention to regions of the world where people first engaged in novel practices like cultivating and domesticating plants and animals, living in towns and then cities, organizing themselves into chiefdoms and then states. The advent of writing is considered the point at which "prehistory" gives way to "history," after which the study of artifacts (in so-called historical archaeology) is often treated as ancillary to learning about the past through textual sources.

To be sure, the broad-brush sequence described in these texts captures core elements of our shared human story. Our earliest human ancestors are found in Africa. Evidence the world over demonstrates that stone technologies preceded metals. Human ancestors hunted and gathered before they produced food by cultivating plants and raising animals. However, this way of telling "our" human story leaves out much that is learned through archaeology. A preoccupation with first instances in standard prehistory texts conveys the impression that human history is a race, implying that it matters who "got there first." They treat the past of select areas of the world as stand-ins for all, elevating particular sequences to stand for the universal. By shining the spotlight of prehistory on select regions, they leave others in the shadows. In other words, they create a norm against which the past of other parts of the world is deemed, at best, different, but more often "late to the party" and therefore behind. It does not require great reflection to see how these ways of recounting "prehistory" perpetuate colonial notions that some regions and groups of people are more progressive, more complex, more modern, than others.

These narratives ignore the varied paths through which people invented or adopted similar practices or arrived at alternatives in different global areas. Neither cities nor trade, farming nor hunting-gathering looks the same the world over, as archaeological evidence shows. Neither do the variety of lifeways represented on the planet today capture the range of our forebears' ones. Simply projecting present variation into the past in the fashion of Sir John Lubbock or as depicted in Figure 3 ignores the complexity and variation of past lifeways. This dusty history of archaeology matters today because the simplistic progressive story it helped to create is enshrined in school texts and carried forward in popular media – films, video games, tourist brochures – despite the fact that archaeologists over recent decades have repeatedly discussed its pitfalls and how it glosses over the rich insights gained through archaeological research.[4]

If archaeology aided the development of 19th-century social evolutionary perspectives and carried them forward in 20th-century presentations of world archaeology, why should we care about archaeology today? What is its value in the 21st century? Archaeology matters because its material evidence (in the form of things and the contexts in which they occur) is our primary source for learning about most of human history (Chapter 1). It illuminates how people the world over confronted universal human challenges: how to feed and care for their families; organize themselves into communities; interact with their neighbors and settle disagreements; tap into resources without exhausting them; and respond to environmental change caused by climatic cycles, among others. Learning about how past people dealt with these issues helps us to understand the shape of our world today and provides clues to how we might respond to similar challenges. In short, archaeology can provide the stuff of future possibilities (Chapter 5). Doing so effectively requires that archaeologists expand our understanding through a combination of new data and critically attuned use of analogy as part of our systematic scientific methodologies.

Over the last half century, archaeologists have grappled with how to use analogy effectively to explore the variety of human experience and ingenuity through time. Analogy remains central to how archaeologists "come to know." However, today archaeologists know that analogy provides hypotheses that must be compared with archaeological data, learning from both how things are similar and how they differ. Rather than exporting what we know from recent times based on one or two points of similarity with past contexts, contemporary archaeologists recognize the need to establish points of similarity and difference empirically and then use points of difference to prise open new understandings. So too must archaeologists be attuned to anachronisms if they are to avoid projecting features characteristic of later times into earlier times. Here, a working knowledge of recent colonial histories is important, even for archaeologists who study so-called "prehistory." As colonial history makes clear, new and arbitrary boundaries were imposed on groups of people through European colonization. Colonial overrule led to changes in daily practice. It affected where people lived, what they produced and consumed, how they dressed, with whom they interacted and married, their structures of family and governance, and more. Virgin soil epidemics, caused by diseases newly introduced to regions where people lacked immunity, devastated populations in the Americas and elsewhere. Naïvely projecting colonial-period social boundaries and practices onto a deeper past ignores the complexities of these histories and the dynamism of the communities involved. Doing so also ignores sustained connections that linked communities on a continental and intercontinental basis, some going back centuries and indeed millennia, as we shall see in Chapter 3.

Other Ways of Knowing

An important way that archaeologists today expand understanding of past lifeways is by taking seriously non-European ways of knowing and being. Here we need to consider what scholars call "epistemology" and "ontology." These fancy words refer to "ways of knowing" and "ways of being," respectively. Importantly, epistemologies and ontologies are plural things – they differ across societies. Broadly characterized, modern western epistemology and ontology carry forward perspectives developed in Renaissance times, honed during the Enlightenment, and solidified through the course of the Industrial Revolution. This intellectual genealogy (see note 3, this chapter) shaped foundational principles of contemporary western common sense (a shared way of knowing and being), including:

- a tendency to treat mind and body as separate, with the mind viewed as a seat of wisdom and knowledge;
- a view that humans are exceptional in their intelligence and therefore stand apart from and in hierarchical relation to other organic lifeforms;
- a confidence that we can distinguish phenomena as natural or cultural and that cultural phenomena can be assigned to layer-cake-like realms of the material/technological, social, and ideological, with technology as a foundational layer;
- an assumption that human history is ordered by progress, understood as synonymous with "improvement" (since the 19th century, technology has been seen as a singular source of progress and a means by which humans solve problems and overcome nature);

- an emphasis on individuals, their needs and desires, over communities/collectives.

To be sure, western scholars have debated these principles, but a rapid scan of modern institutions helps us to appreciate how they influence ways of learning and being. In universities, separate departments study the mind (psychology) and body (biology/medicine). Social sciences study human societies while animals are studied within the sciences. Museums were long structured by the distinction between history and natural history. History museums were the place to learn about literate/civilized society, and natural history museums the place to learn about non/preliterate societies and animals. Here again we see how categories of typological time shaped the carving up of knowledge domains.

Without a doubt, western ways of knowing and being provide important and reliable insights into the world around us. But they are not the only or at all times best source of insight. Other societies have flourished through different ways of knowing and being, and recent decades have seen attention paid by western scholars to how other perspectives transform what and how we know. Consider, for example, how health practices and medicine are expanded through other-than-European perspectives on the relationship between mind and body (think yoga, meditation, acupuncture). Similarly, many archaeologists today appreciate how taking into account other ways of knowing and being enriches understanding of human history and past lifeways.

This takes us back to analogy. When we consider the world around us through the lens of other epistemologies and ontologies (ways of knowing and being), we enlarge possibilities by having a wider set of referents through which to gauge similarities and differences, present and past. Archaeology offers many examples of how this expands interpretive possibilities. For instance, early scholars who studied ancient rock art assumed that the animals painted by ancient artists reflected what people ate. However, when archaeologists working in southern Africa compared animals painted by ancient artists with animal bones from associated sites, they found a mismatch. This suggested that rock art did not reflect prehistoric menus, and led a group of scholars to explore practices through which humans and non-human beings relate among historically recent societies.

In southern Africa, rock art researchers looked to descriptions of 19th- and 20th-century Kalahari San hunter-gatherer communities who forge connections with animals and far-away family and community members through trance dancing. Used as a comparative analogy, these practices aligned well with ancient rock art images of people standing in circles, hands clapping, and depicted with physical signs of being in a trance state (specific body postures and bleeding from the nose). Animals depicted in the rock paintings are more convincingly interpreted as ones associated with trancing practices rather than dining practices. But comparisons also revealed differences, for example in the kinds of animals featured in the rock art across different southern African regions. These differences lent insight into how trancing varied across space and through time.[5]

Rock art studies have seen vigorous debate over whether trancing practices like those of historic African San communities provide clues for interpreting more ancient European Paleolithic rock art. Spirals and dots are geometric motifs recurrently seen by people experiencing hallucinations, and some archaeologists argue that their presence in painted caves of France, Spain, and elsewhere suggest that the ancient creators of Paleolithic rock art may have had similar trance-induced experiences. Other archaeologists disagree, pointing to distinctions and differences between the rock art of southern Africa and Pleistocene Europe. But there is little doubt that knowledge about historic San ways of knowing and being has expanded interpretive possibilities. Like all analogies, however, they prove convincing only when subject to comparison with archaeological evidence, assessing points of similarity and difference and treating differences as starting points for new questions and deeper understanding of how life in the past varied over time.

North America's Pacific Northwest offers an example of how archaeologists enrich interpretation by considering a wider set of foundational premises (ontologies). Here, seasonal runs of salmon were central to Indigenous lifeways. Archaeologists schooled in western ways of knowing characterized these communities as settled "hunter-gatherers" and studied their use of fish as a "subsistence adaptation." Guided in part by historic accounts of Indigenous fishing techniques, archaeologists found remains of ancient wood and stone traps and weirs used to catch fish as they moved to river spawning grounds. Some of these features have been radiocarbon dated to thousands of years ago, providing important evidence for the longevity of fishing lifeways. By identifying species represented among fish bones at associated settlements, archaeologists have shown that Indigenous people harvested an array of species in addition to salmon, which researchers had assumed to be the primary focus of fishing. Evidence like this proves important to contemporary Indigenous communities, faced with having to demonstrate to government officials who make decisions about contemporary fishing rights that these are long-lived practices protected by treaty rights.

Our understanding of past lifeways is deepened when archaeologists value Indigenous ways of knowing and being as sources of insight. As anthropologists have underscored over recent decades, communities of people who live by hunting and gathering understand their world as shaped by relationships – not only with other humans but also with non-human persons, which include animals and other animate beings. Earlier scholars treated these relationships as metaphors, but many today understand these as foundational principles of how humans, animals, and technology interact. Rather than merely an economic act (with intent to feed the family), fishing involved social interaction between humans and other sentient beings, in this case fish, together with the technologies through which humans gained access to fish. Archaeologist Robert Losey describes how this insight expands understanding of a recurrent pattern seen among ancient fish weirs in what is today the state of Washington.[6] In documenting weirs between 500 and 2,000 years old, archaeologists observed that, despite evidence of recurrent rebuilding and reuse, all weirs were partial. None could effectively trap fish in the form they were when archaeologists mapped them.

Preservation factors like erosion or organic decay could account for why weir parts were missing. Losey considers these possibilities, but cites evidence for why such explanations are not convincing when compared to the archaeological contexts. Instead, he sees the pattern of partial preservation as best accounted for by people intentionally dismantling weirs when not in use. This, he argues, relates to how Indigenous people conceived their relationships with fish. Fish are understood as sentient beings and their relationship with people depends upon respectful reciprocal gestures. Fish offer themselves up as food for people, but people are responsible for actions that regenerate fish communities. Linguistic evidence points to a relationship between weirs and houses among some communities, with the implication that, just as protocol demanded that a host be home to welcome and care for guests, so too should weirs only invite visits with a host present. Partially dismantling the weirs when not in use ensured that fish were not trapped if humans were not there to harvest them and practice the reciprocal gestures that ensured fish well-being.

While this might be understood today as "conservation," Losey argues that Indigenous ontology helps us to appreciate a mode of interaction between humans and animals based on networks of interdependence rather than functional explanations of cause and effect. In doing so, these perspectives widen our appreciation of possibilities, past, present, and future, a point to which I return in Chapter 5. Losey's use of analogy takes the form of what philosopher Alison Wylie terms a "tacking" back and forth between an archaeological context and an ethnographically described practice.[7] Drawing on multiple lines of evidence (archaeological, linguistic, geological, and ethnographic), he is careful to compare and evaluate points of similarity and difference between past and present contexts.

In another example of how an archaeology attuned to Indigenous practice has contributed to new understandings of the past with present-day significance, we turn to the Amazon basin. Occupying an area roughly the size of the contiguous United States or Europe, the Amazon is the world's largest drainage system. Its once extensive forests play a key role in global climate regulation, but recent human action like timbering and clearing these forests for farming and mining has imperiled this awesome ecosystem. We err, however, if we imagine the Amazon as a place that has only seen substantive human presence in the last century or two – treating it as reservoir of biodiversity untouched by humans – and here is where archaeology makes an important contribution to expanding understanding of the forms and consequences of human activity.

An image of the Amazon basin as a place largely uninhabited by people emerged through late 19th- and early 20th-century accounts of travelers, missionaries, and early anthropologists. Their accounts characterized the region's Indigenous societies as few in number and eking out an existence in difficult environments. These descriptions led mid-20th-century anthropologist Betty Meggers to argue that the Amazonian environment limited the development of agriculture and therefore political complexity among Amazonian societies. Her work prompted vigorous debate over the size of populations that could be supported by Indigenous agricultural systems, which combined extensive (shifting or so-called swidden) manioc cultivation with foods obtained through hunting, fishing, collecting, and agroforestry. It also prompted debate over the extent of post-Columbian depopulation resulting from disease and colonial violence.[8]

Today, thanks to the results of interdisciplinary research known as historical ecology, our picture of life in the ancient Amazon is much different.[9] Historical ecology brings together research from archaeology, geography, soil science ecology, ethnography, and history to study interactions of species, including humans, and their environments over long periods. A key feature of this research is its focus on landscapes rather than individual sites or settlements. Only by considering settlements in relation to the range of locations and resources that shaped people's daily lives in times past can we appreciate how today's landscapes were shaped in turn by people's actions and relationships.

The picture that emerges is of landscapes transformed through the daily actions of generations of Indigenous Amazonian communities. Geographer William Denevan was among the first to draw attention to extensive and expansive pre-Columbian earthworks in the Llanos de Moxos region of Bolivia.[10] Flying over the area in a small aircraft in 1961, Denevan suspected that mounds, canals, ring ditches, and forest islands visible from the air were traces of human action on the landscape. Their specific forms vary across the Amazon's wide expanses, but as interdisciplinary research has shown, there is ample evidence that ancient Amazonians engineered landscapes through terrascaping, creating organic-rich so-called dark earths, and shaping the composition of forest biota.

Data from archaeology, paleogeography, and historical ecology reveal a complex history of interaction of people, landscape, and biota in Amazonia and elsewhere. People domesticate landscapes through a range of actions. Clearing land for settlement creates edge environments that attract new plant and animal species. People intentionally and unintentionally introduce new species. Burning can further open areas and add nutrients to soil. Longer-term settlements add organic and inorganic materials to soils, forming dark earths, which concentrate valuable nutrients that can be tapped by future cultivators. In Amazonia, landscape cultivation led to enduring modifications to the earth's surface as people created mounds, dug ditches to alter water flow, and changed soil composition through additives. They selectively cleared vegetation to establish gardens or fields, leaving desirable tree species to grow and encouraging opportunities for other plants. We have evidence that ancient Amazonians selectively encouraged trees of the palm family (Arecaceae) to grow as species valued for their fruits, wood, and fronds. Scholars debate the extent of landscape modification and its variation across the massive Amazon basin, which ongoing aerial LiDAR mapping continues to reveal. However, there is wide agreement that archaeology has yielded new insight into the role of the region's Indigenous people in creating the biodiverse ecosphere which is today threatened by rampant forest clearance.[11]

Accustomed to the styles of landscape cultivation characteristic of their homelands (a source of analogy), Europeans were blind to the many forms of landscape modification and management practiced by people living in the Americas, Africa, and elsewhere, particularly among people whom Europeans categorized as "hunter-gatherers" or "foragers." Archaeology provides important evidence for these practices. Returning to the Pacific Northwest, archaeological evidence is today lending insight into how Indigenous communities promoted conditions that benefited the growth of resources on which they relied, whether through periodic burning of landscapes to promote growth of camas – a native bulb valued as a food source – and valued trees or through building of intertidal structures that promoted growth of clams (so-called clam gardens).[12]

Archaeology helps us to appreciate the continuum of relationships between humans, plants, animals, and landscapes that the term "domestication" masks. In its widely understood sense, domesticated animals and plants differ from their wild ancestors in ways that benefit humans (think large fruits like apples, or tame milk cows). Domestication is understood as laying the foundation for agricultural and herding economies and resulting from conscious human selection (like interbreeding). However, interdisciplinary research among plant and animal scientists, geneticists, and archaeologists reveals the diverse pathways through which humans, non-human animals, and plants developed mutualistic relationships. These span a continuum ranging from full dependency (maize seeds so tightly enclosed that cobs must be husked for them to germinate) to more symmetrical relations (like those between reindeer and their Sámi herders). While we can point to contemporary examples (analogies) for a range of these practices, archaeological evidence expands our appreciation of their scale (e.g., in the Amazon basin), sustainability over long periods, and different pathways through which humans, plants, animals, and landscapes interacted through time.[13]

In these ways, archaeology addresses pressing issues of today. Archaeological sites provide direct evidence for ancient biodiversity in the form of animal bones and plant remains studied for their potential to yield ancient DNA and insights into species identification and history. Archaeology helps us to appreciate how humans interacted with plants and animals to create niches and developed practices that sustained or sometimes eroded those niches. While ancient examples do not provide direct parallels for the challenges of sustainability and food security we face today, they can provide useful analogies (applied in reverse: from past to present) as tools for thinking. The foreign country that is the past and the different ways in which people did things there – to echo Hartley's often-cited line (see opening quote, this chapter) – lend an important perspective as we reflect on present and future times, a topic to which we return in Chapter 5.

In sum, archaeology matters because it supplies primary material evidence for human history in temporal scales ranging from intimate to vast. As we have seen, recognizing deep-time history hinged on finding ancient stone tools and recognizing them as such. We have also seen that coming to know about past lifeways involves tacking back and forth between archaeology's material sources and fuller knowledge of the world as we know it. Thus, time and knowing are linked through use of analogy in archaeological inquiry. When used illustratively to animate rather than interrogate past contexts, analogy anachronistically projects contemporary and historic lifeways into the past. However, when we cast our epistemological and ontological nets wide and use analogy comparatively, it helps us to understand commonalities and differences among past lifeways across vast geographies and varied time scales using archaeology's material evidence. Doing so effectively depends on how we approach those materials, as we shall take up next.

3

Connections through Things

Don't read what we have written; look at what we have done.

> James Deetz, *In Small Things Forgotten: An Archaeology of Early American Life* (New York: Anchor Books, 1977), p. 161

Pause to look around. Whether reading at home, in a library, or on public transportation, objects to which you give passing notice surround you. We call these things tools, technology, equipment, furniture, ornaments, clothing, and so on. Made from an array of materials and formed through techniques about which we know little, some are ordinary, others ornate. Some are durable. We resist disposing of some of them because of their cost or significance. Others we deem disposable. Some we discard or pass along through sale, trade, or donation. Some are taken from us. Others we lose. In time, some will come to rest in places where future archaeologists may find them.

Regardless, these things have histories: they were made somewhere by someone using techniques passed down through generations. Whether we recognize it or not, things carry traces of connections: to where they were made, how they arrived, where they were used, how they were used, by whom, and with what effects. In short, things are crucial elements of our social lives and each has a story – what scholars call an itinerary or a biography.

From the early 20th century, anthropologists and archaeologists referred to things used by people as "material culture." Linguists call this a "marked" term. Marking signals difference from a word's standard meaning. Here, "material" marks "culture," which is typically understood as being about customs, beliefs, and social practices (of which more in Chapter 4). The fact that scholars used a marked term to signal *made* things (artifacts) reveals an assumption about their role in social life. Western scholarship has tended to prioritize thoughts and ideas over things. We imagine things as outcomes of ideas or mental templates. In this way, we privilege mind over material and treat things as backdrops to our social interactions. This implies that culture comes before and is impressed on the material world – culture is made material. In other words, things are treated as *reflecting* rather than actively *constituting* culture.

This way of thinking about things is not universal – it has a history, grounded in ideas touched on in Chapter 2. Many societies (including pre-Renaissance European ones) accord things greater agency, and scholars across a range of fields have begun to study how things shape human lives.[1] Some use the term "materiality" to signal this shift. Whether or not they use this fancy word, many scholars today argue that what we call "culture" emerges *through* our relationships with things and materials. Things work on and with us to produce effects, whether by transforming raw materials into finished products, producing our gendered, ethnic, and class identities, or transforming a place from a mundane to a sacred space. As implied in the words of archaeologist James Deetz that opened this chapter, things are crucial components of – and agents in – the everyday activities that make us who we are. Through their materials, attributes, design, and histories, things shape human action.

Consider a chair. Its materials and form encourage particular ways of sitting: erectly and alertly in an upright classroom seat or in more relaxed fashion in a living room chair. Though designed for sitting, a chair also affords the opportunity to stack books or collect tossed-off clothes (unless the chair happens to be a throne). So while we might use something close to hand for a different purpose than intended by design, its form and attributes suggest potential uses and channel actions.

In doing so, not all objects act on us in the same way. Some set standards, as archaeologist John Robb describes.[2] These things generally escape day-to-day notice, but are linked to doing things "right." Examples include conventions of dress, décor, and the layout of houses or public buildings. We mostly notice them when they depart from a prevailing standard, which things subtly convey, reinforce, and negotiate. Think for a moment about how fashion acts on us. We notice new styles for their difference, which recedes as they become conventional. The pace of these cycles has quickened in recent times, but the ways in which objects act on us to set standards is a general feature of human social life.

Other objects draw attention. They stand out for the skill involved in their making, their rarity, among other qualities. Meant to be noticed, these things have the power to distinguish: for example, luxury goods. Status is made and maintained by possessing them. If they become more available and widely circulated, their power to distinguish lessens and new elite forms take their place. Again, we are familiar with this cycle today, but it is a recurrent feature of human–thing relations throughout history.

Still other objects guide memory and create connections through time, serving as meaningful actors in the recounting of history or ritual performance. Some mediate relations between humans and other beings like ancestors and spirits. These things are often deemed sacred and inalienable, with the irony that museums and private art collections around the world are filled with them. Their vitality as cultural property has put such things at the center of long-fought repatriation struggles: for example, those concerning wampum belts fashioned from marine shell beads and central to Algonkian and Iroquoian social and political alliances and ceremonialism.[3]

Though the specific forms of standard-setting, distinction-making, or memory-making things vary through time and across cultural contexts, the point is that we fashion ourselves through things. People and things are mutually constituted. As such, objects *matter* in social life. Stripped of the things that humans create and acquire to enhance their lives, the stories of our lives and histories are radically incomplete.

Connections through Things

By studying things (artifacts, features, and monuments) and their contexts, archaeology helps us to appreciate the dynamic relationships between humans, materials, and things through time. In this way, you could say that archaeology *matters* history. Though popular works on archaeology foreground pyramids, temples, and monuments, much of what we learn as archaeologists comes from studying humble objects used in everyday lives. James Deetz referred to these as "small things forgotten," echoing a phrase used in probate inventories by New England Puritans as a catch-all for miscellaneous items with negligible value. In his influential book of the same title quoted at the head of this chapter, he made an impassioned case for how attention to things expanded understanding of daily life in colonial New England.

As an historical archaeologist, Deetz drew on documents and archaeological materials to explore changes in New Englanders' lifeways over the 17th and 18th centuries. Probate inventories of the time were very detailed, some even listing possessions room by room. Deetz used them to study how houses were furnished, how people dressed, their tools and equipment, and how they organized daily activities. When combined with evidence for architectural changes drawn from archaeology and textual sources, probate inventories reflect key changes in the organization of daily activity during that century. Rooms took on specialized functions, becoming less multi-purpose; floor plans and dwelling exteriors became more symmetrical; and households had more and a greater variety of tableware as people began to eat from individual place settings rather than eating and drinking from shared vessels. Deetz argued that these material differences reflected a changing "world view," but archaeologists today argue that things like individualized place settings at the dinner table play an active role in creating and reinforcing an ethos of individualism. In other words, we are *how* we eat.

Engaging the World through Things

Things and technologies shape who we become and how we engage the world in ways that scientists are just beginning to understand. Think here of ongoing neuroscience studies of how digital media and technologies affect our brains, cognition, and behavior. While we may think that digital technologies are exceptional, there is cause to ask how earlier things and technologies affected perception and cognition. A case in point is the "perspectival revolution" associated with times commonly referred to as the European Renaissance and Scientific Revolution. Lenses used in telescopes and microscopes produced new ways of seeing. So did the innovation of creating a vanishing point in drawing and painting. This pictorial device lent three-dimensionality to drawings and paintings, fostering a new relationship between viewer and image by locating the viewer in space. Our understanding of these innovations is aided by textual sources, but archaeologists also study the relationship between things and sensory perception in earlier times.

In *How Ancient Europeans Saw the World*, archaeologist Peter Wells makes the case for how recurrent patterning in the form, shape, decoration, and design of things (pottery, personal ornaments, weapons, graves) reveals changing "ways of seeing" during Bronze and Iron Age times across central and western Europe. Two fundamental shifts in the look of things took place: one in the 5th century BCE and another several centuries later. In analyzing these, Wells makes the case that some of the visual strategies used to grab our attention in advertising and media today were used with effect during ancient times.

Before the first shift, communities during Later Bronze Age and Early Iron Age times emphasized straight lines and symmetrically arranged geometric shapes (squares, triangles, circles) in decorating locally made pottery, brooches (fibulae), swords, scabbards, and other things. Over the course of the 5th century BCE, these gave way to asymmetrical eye-catching curvilinear designs like those of the well-known La Tène style. In this and related styles, emphasis on S-lines and spirals guides vision in a different way. At the same time, the naturalized depictions of animals seen in earlier times were succeeded by ones that combined different animal elements to create hybrid "monsters." Wells argues that these curvilinear elements and unusual animals "were designed ... to make people look, to attract and hold their attention, to engage them in fascination and puzzle solving."[4]

These visual design changes coincided with ritual changes. Ritual performance in earlier times centered on the burial of elites whose graves were equipped with many and carefully arranged objects: cauldrons, drinking vessels, swords, and scabbards. By Late Iron Age times, ritual focused instead on ditched enclosures in which archaeologists find evidence of feasting, together with large numbers of bent and broken weapons (swords, scabbards, lance points).

Taken together, Wells argues that these adjustments in design and ritual relate to widening social connections and shifting community concerns from the Early to Middle Iron Age. Occasionally, goods from afar have been found on Bronze and Early Iron Age sites in temperate Europe, but from about the 6th century BCE Middle Iron Age communities participated in an expanding interaction sphere. People were exposed to things drawn from a broader geographical range, including objects of ivory, bronze, and silk sourced from the Mediterranean basin and beyond. New visual styles circulated, together with new things like bronze mirrors, which became more widely distributed from the 5th century BCE. Communities varied in how they mobilized elements drawn from this varied geographical pool. But a common thread across temperate Europe was a shift in how communities related to local elites – as reflected in those elaborately laid-out early graves – with people becoming more preoccupied with their relationships to a wider world enacted through design elements and new forms of ritual centered on ditched enclosures.

During the 2nd century BCE, the visual world of Late Iron Age peoples was remade again, this time through technological changes and expanding participation in interregional and intercontinental commerce. Pottery was now often wheel-made, more standardized and more simply decorated with vertical lines. Things like brooches/fibulae were mass-made and less ornate. S-curves largely disappeared from the visual repertoire. Coins joined the range of serially manufactured objects that now formed the visual field of things. Taken together, Wells argues that these changes relate to the development of a "new, world-commercially based mode of visualization more than a century before Caesar led his legions into Gaul in 58 BC."[5] Throughout these many centuries, Wells argues that things and their visual qualities participated in remaking how people related to one another and shaped their experience of changing connections to a wider world.

Connections through Small Things: Beads as Social Technology

Among the small things with notable effects on our social lives are bodily ornaments. People everywhere adorn their bodies in ways that express, communicate, and produce social connections and distinctions. Beads are primary among technologies of adornment and one of the earliest durable forms of decorative art and symbolic expression used by humans. As early as 120,000 years ago, modern humans living in the Levant collected and strung naturally perforated shells. Wear on the shells suggests that they were used as bodily ornaments. Archaeologists have found small deliberately perforated shells from about 75,000 years ago in Middle Stone Age (Blombos) cave deposits in southern Africa, which carried traces of red ochre, whether applied directly to the beads or to the bodies they adorned. They have also found ochre-stained ostrich eggshell beads in contexts dated to 31,000 years ago in China, underscoring the geographically widespread and ancient human preoccupation with bodily ornamentation.

Paleoanthropologists who study early human lifeways argue that beads and other ornaments were important in creating connections among geographically dispersed people, like Paleolithic communities living a mobile lifestyle based on hunting and gathering. By means of their visual qualities, ornaments operated as an "information technology" through which social connections and differences were forged.[6] Moreover, bodily ornaments are widely understood cross-culturally not simply as "decorations," but also as things linked to personhood, identity, and well-being. In short, they are social technologies. To illustrate how archaeologists use these small things to develop important insights into past lifeways, let's journey through time and across space to consider the social lives of beads.

Beads and other forms of personal adornment often participate in making social distinction. Early and spectacular examples come from the site of Sunghir, located 200 km northeast of Moscow, Russia.[7] First excavated in the mid-1960s, these Upper Paleolithic burials date to about 30,000–34,000 years ago and are the oldest securely dated modern human burials in the world. Three stand out for their spectacular adornment. Sunghir 1 was a mature male, aged 35–45 years old at death. An unhealed spinal wound suggests that he died from a stone spear blow, though whether he was wounded in a hunting accident or a fight is impossible to say. However he died, he was treated specially by those who buried him. His body was covered with red ochre and buried with about 3,000 mammoth ivory beads, some sewn onto clothing, others strung and placed on his arms, chest, knees, and ankles. On his head were 12 pierced fox teeth, perhaps sewn onto a cap, and his arms were adorned with 25 mammoth ivory bangles. The ivory beads alone required an estimated 2,000–3,000 hours of labour to make, suggesting that those who laid him to rest esteemed the man.

Another grave held two young individuals (Sunghir 2 and 3) buried head-to-head. Their teeth showed signs that they experienced developmental stress as they grew. One (Sunghir 3) had bowed upper legs, his bones showing signs of arrested growth. The other had unusual dental and cranial features. Despite being only around 10 years old at death, both were heavily adorned, each with about 5,000 mammoth ivory beads, probably sewn onto their clothing. Sunghir 2 also had some 300 fox canines as part of a cap and belt. Both wore mammoth ivory bangles on their arms, and parts of their bodies were covered in ochre. Sixteen mammoth ivory spears were buried alongside these young people. With these individuals having died so young, some archaeologists suggest that their elaborate burial reflects a status inherited rather than achieved, but it may equally relate to their unusual physical features. Regardless, the astonishing array of ornaments with which these individuals were buried would have had a marked effect on those who laid their bodies to rest, perhaps with the intent that the effect would carry into the afterlife.

From the time of their earliest uses in Middle and Upper Paleolithic times, beads have been widely embraced as a medium for social interaction and creativity. Though their specific uses varied across space and through time, they share qualities that have given them universal appeal as a social technology that shapes people's relations with each other and perhaps also with non-human beings (rosaries being a familiar example). In this regard, beads can be potent substances valued for their efficacy in ritual actions and as items of exchange. They can be made from a range of materials – stone, clay, bone, shell, and more recently glass – and examples from wide-ranging periods and geographical contexts point to their active role in social interactions and transactions. Small and portable, beads made from marine shell and stone were moved by people over exceptionally long distances from Paleolithic times onward, with value assigned to their varying colors and sources in specific cultural contexts. They were thus objects that could distinguish, attract attention, set standards, and produce connections through time and across geographies.

The development of glass-making technology some 4,000 years ago was profoundly consequential for beads and for the intercontinental connections created through their exchange in the millennia since. Early centers of glass- and bead-making emerged in different areas of the world at different times: Mesopotamia and Egypt by 1400 BCE; the Indian subcontinent by the 3rd century BCE; Syria in pre-Roman times; the Yorùbá region of what is today Nigeria from at least the early second millennium CE; and Venice from Renaissance times, among others. Early glass bead-making often mimicked the colors of precious and semi-precious stones already valued as sources of social distinction in ancient societies, for example lapis lazuli's intense blue. However, the many ways to vary glass through its fabrication – by adding different minerals and controlling furnace conditions – widened the range of bead colors, further enhancing their potential as sources for social creativity.

Over the millennia since, glass beads have become key elements in the artistic traditions of communities around the world, augmenting and at other times substituting for previously used resources. As an example, Indigenous North American communities extended their repertoire of textile decoration over recent centuries by using small glass beads – called seed beads – as substitutes for the dyed porcupine quills used in quillwork. Ndebele, Xhosa, Nguni, and other southern African communities incorporated seed beads into elaborately decorated skirts and neck collars formerly decorated with shells, feathers, seeds, and metal beads. These examples demonstrate a recurrent feature of long-standing global exchange: that people take up imported goods for their own purposes and use them in ways shaped by their histories rather than by the intentions of those who produced and exchanged them.

We will return to this question of uptake (or "consumption") below, but by way of background, first recognize that there is more than one way to make both glass and glass beads. A commonly used base material is silica/sand, but its high melting point requires use of a flux like soda or potash to lower its melting temperature, together with stabilizers like lime to enhance glass durability. Different additives – lead, iron, cobalt, copper, gold, and others – affect glass color and transparency, as do furnace conditions like the amount of oxygen available during heating. Glass beads can be formed by drawing, winding, blowing, or molding. Drawn beads are cut from long (drawn) glass tubes and finished by heating or grinding to make individual beads. Some tubes are a single color, but complex designs are made by layering different glass colors or adding decorations by incising, stamping, or other means. To make a wound bead, a thin filament of glass is wrapped around a solid (usually metal) core called a mandrel.

Out of these many choices and possibilities, glass-making regions opted for specific glass recipes and bead-makers tended to specialize in a single way of forming beads. Scholars call these combinations of choices a "technological style." These styles were learned, honed, and modified by groups of people who worked together in specific locations – whether individual workshops in Venice or regions like southern India, where glass bead-making was common for centuries. Importantly, individual beads carry traces of all these technical choices: the recipes used to make and color glass and the techniques used to form and finish beads. In short, glass beads come in a dizzying array of forms that reflect long histories of manufacturing in different centers around the world, from the famous guilds of Venice to those in Bohemia, Egypt, India, Nigeria, China, and elsewhere.

Over recent decades, new analytical techniques have revolutionized our ability to conduct non-destructive source analyses on glass (among other things). Lasers generate tiny particles that are ionized and analyzed using mass spectrometry to identify a material's chemical elements and isotopes. Known as Laser Ablation Inductively Coupled Plasma Mass Spectrometry (LA-ICP-MS), this analytical technique lends new insight into worldwide trade in raw glass and finished beads over millennia. When combined with careful analysis of bead-making techniques (whether drawn, wound, or molded), and the paths through which they were distributed, consumed, and ultimately deposited in locations where archaeologists find them – in other words, by studying their itineraries – glass beads have proven a rich source of insight into the over-sized role of these small finds in forging connections within and between continents.

West Africa is a region well known for the vast quantities of European-manufactured glass beads imported there throughout the Atlantic slave trade period (late 15th–19th centuries CE). During the 20th century, archaeologists often treated glass beads as important primarily for determining the age of sites – sites with known styles of trade beads could be dated based on periods of manufacture. However, recent research reveals a far more complex history of glass and glass beads across West Africa, including a vibrant trade across the Sahara desert that brought both stone and glass beads into the subcontinent from the 7th century CE if not earlier. For centuries, communities across the Mediterranean exchanged copper and copper alloys (the metal being rare in West Africa), salt, beads, and cloth, among other commodities, in order to access gold, kola, nuts, and slaves from this part of the continent. Sourcing studies show that beads made from glass fabricated in Mesopotamia, Egypt, and the Levantine coast made their way into communities across West Africa during the many centuries of trans-Saharan trade. Ancient cities along the Niger River and its now-dry tributaries – entrepôts like Timbuktu, Essouk, and Gao – were conduits for trade in glass beads that ultimately reached even modest-sized communities in places like Senegal, far to the west. In short, glass beads circulated widely over the last 1,400 years and were put to a range of social uses.

Europeans were motivated to undertake 15th-century maritime exploration of West Africa's coasts by a desire to access the region's gold directly. While maritime traffic in gold and ivory continued for centuries, there was a rapid shift to a focus on slaves exported in a growing Atlantic triangular trade: Europeans brought goods to Africa to acquire slaves, who were exported to provide labor for expanding plantation production across the Americas, and were used to produce raw materials and generate wealth that sustained colonies and their European metropoles. This trade fueled (what was eventually) industrial production in Europe and the Americas, alongside new forms of consumption worldwide.[8] Glass beads were among manufactured things that became staples of post-Columbian exchange, circulating widely through Atlantic trade with consequential effects.

But not all glass beads came from glass-making centers in Europe. From the 17th century, an eye-catching type of blue glass bead sometimes referred to as "Aggrey" or "Akori" came to the attention of European merchants operating along West Africa's Guinea coast. Purchased along the Benin Bight, these beads were resold by merchants along the Gold Coast (today Ghana) to the west, but their source was long debated. It was nonetheless clear that they were highly valued across West Africa and known particularly for how they changed color. Held in the hand, they look blue; viewed against the light, they are green-yellow. In other words, they are dichroic.

Recent research at the famed site of Ilé Ifè located in the forested region of what is today southwestern Nigeria has recast understanding about ancient glass- and bead-making in this part of the world. The centuries-old city is revered as the ancestral home of Yorùbá people who share mutually intelligible languages, cultural practices, and history. Ilé Ifè and related sites are renowned for exquisitely crafted naturalistic sculptures of brass, terracotta, and stone dating to the 12th through the 15th century CE. Many are human figures interpreted as portraits of esteemed individuals wearing beaded crowns, together with beaded necklaces and bracelets. These figures echo earlier stone sculptures from around the region, which date to after about 750 CE (called the Late Formative). Late Formative sculptures show naturalistic human figures – male and female – adorned with simple beaded necklaces, bracelets, and anklets. Archaeologists find jasper, carnelian, and other red-brown chalcedonic stone beads on Late Formative and later sites. It seems likely that beads depicted on Late Formative stone sculptures were of such stones, with the closest sources about 400 km to the north along the Niger River. Oral histories make clear that Yorùbá people have long valued these stone beads for their vital force (*àṣẹ*, transformative power and energy) that protects and sustains well-being and is a source of chiefly power.

Stone beads like these retained their prominence as sources of power through the centuries in Yorùbáland. However, in later periods, glass beads were added to the repertoire of powerful paraphernalia valued by Yorùbá chiefs and elites, fueling demand for beaded attire, as seen in Classic period sculptures (Figure 4). Archaeologist Akin Ogundiran describes how Ilé Ifè's reputation as the founding center for all later Yorùbá polities – and there were many – emerged through its monopoly on production of socially valued glass beads and the closely held knowledge behind this technology.[9]

Figure 4. Figure of a king adorned with beads,
Wunmonije site, Ilé Ifè, Nigeria, c. early 14th century
CE. Copper alloy. Height: 37 cm. National Museums,
Lagos. Museum registration no. 13, then 79.R.9.
Renumbered 38.1.1. Photo courtesy of Akinwumi
Ogundiran and with permission of National
Commission of Monuments and Museums, Nigeria.

Early scholars assumed that glass bead-making at Ilé Ifè was based on the re-melting and reworking of glass imported from the Mediterranean world and beyond. However, recent research shows that workshops in the city made beads from locally produced glass using a distinctive high-lime, high-alumina recipe (HLHA for short) for which granitic sand was a primary raw material. Powdered snail shell was added as a stabilizer and Ilé Ifè's skilled workers made drawn-glass beads in a range of colors – including blue dichroic – on an industrial scale from at least the 12th through the 15th centuries. The highly valued beads fabricated here circulated widely across West Africa for many centuries. Drawing insight from oral histories, proverbs, color symbolism, and archaeological contexts, Ogundiran argues that Ilé Ifè's beads were "more than [just] things." They were a source of vitality and form of social capital that became "an indispensable representation of social order and wellness, and therefore ... an object and a subject of ultimate desire."[10] During the Classical period of Yorùbá history (1000–1420 CE), glass beads came to be central to life processes ranging from fertility and well-being in childhood to puberty and marriage, alongside the role they played as chiefly prestige goods. Through its monopoly on production of these highly valued objects and associated knowledge, Ilé Ifè materialized into Yorùbáland's primal center.

These early circulations of stone and glass beads throughout West Africa created the context for circulations and consumption of European-made glass beads through Atlantic triangular trade. Beads were already valued things when Europeans showed up on West Africa's Guinea coast, just as they were all along the Atlantic seaboard of North America and throughout the Caribbean. European merchants discovered through experience that existing tastes meant that not any imports would do. Influenced by local histories of production, exchange, and consumption, West Africans' value systems shaped clear preferences among goods. Those things that did not suit the region's tastes languished in storehouses, with European merchants reporting to producers the specific kinds of cloth, beads, and other goods that appealed. Producers in Europe adjusted accordingly, creating connected cycles of taste making that conditioned circulations of things throughout the Atlantic world over centuries.[11] Historic colonial contexts offer many examples of how studying small things in out-of-the-way places sheds new light on these processes that we today call globalization. Colonialism is neither a new nor a singular process, with examples from the ancient and modern worlds alike. Colonialism ushers in changed social circumstances that require creativity and experimentation, albeit often under conditions of duress. As archaeologist Chris Gosden observed, "[C]olonial cultures were created by all who participated in them, so that all had agency and social effect, with coloniser and colonised alike being radically changed by the experience."[12] Glass beads were consistently implicated in these processes in ways that can be studied by following their itineraries across an arc of production, exchange, and consumption.

Archaeological research at the Santa Catalina de Guale mission settlement in Spanish La Florida (1595–1680 CE) provides an example of how careful study of beads can shed light on colonial dynamics.[13] Archaeologists recovered tens of thousands of glass beads (69,325) during excavations at this Spanish mission, destroyed during a 1680 attack led by the English and their Indigenous allies. Many were among goods included in graves of Indigenous converts buried beneath the Franciscan mission church. Consistent with expectations of Franciscan burial in the period, individuals were buried with feet facing the altar, arms folded across their chest. But inconsistent with simple shroud burials favored by Franciscans, the more than

200 intact burials beneath the Santa Catalina de Guale church were rich in grave goods, including a wide assortment of religious medals, medallions, and glass beads. Preservation was such that excavators could see how beads were combined into necklaces and attached to clothing. Using a needle, they carefully restrung beads in place, preserving the associations between individual beads and the patterns they formed. This large and well-preserved assemblage of glass beads provides extraordinarily rich insight into their itineraries, ranging from their place and process of manufacture to how they operated in Indigenous converts' social lives.

The beads came from a range of world sources and may have arrived at any point in the settlement's century-long occupation. Among them was a group of distinctive gold-gilded wire-wound glass beads, likely made in Spain. Many other beads came from Venice. Chemical composition and technical details suggest that they were made by several glass-making guilds, and then passed to multiple bead-finishing workshops where glass tubes were cut, polished, and strung. Strings of single bead types and colors from individual workshops were then sold to merchants, many in Seville, from where they shipped to Mexico City, the administrative center of the growing Spanish empire. From there they traveled to St. Augustine, included among goods supplied to the governor of La Florida to support the colony.

Once the beads arrived in Spanish Florida, they were given by missionaries as gifts or payments for goods like maize to Indigenous elites, who in turn redistributed them among their social networks. While it is unclear how beads were used on a daily basis – whether as rosaries or adornment – those included among grave goods make evident that imported strands were dissembled and reassembled in new ways consistent with Indigenous priorities. By analyzing similarities and differences among the beads in individual graves, archaeologist Elliot Blair has been able to identify relationships among people who used similar beads in similar ways.[14] These differences hint at the possibility that these subsets represent groups of people who moved to the mission at different times and from different communities of practice, a concept we take up in Chapter 4.

Though they are small things, beads help to tell the story of Indigenous life at Santa Catalina de Guale mission. The late 16th and early 17th centuries were uncertain times, with Spanish and other European incursions altering the already dynamic Indigenous political landscape. The Spanish presence created opportunities for new alliances and was a source of things both new (like metal tools) and familiar (like beads). The Spanish in La Florida also sought reliable alliances to ensure access to maize and deer hides, which Guale people supplied in quantity. Through these transactions, beads flowed into a mission community "overseen" at most by several friars. Evidence suggests that Guale chiefs understood the missionaries as brokers in their relationship with St. Augustine but subordinate to them in all but religious matters. At the same time, the mission community grew because of disease and warfare, with survivors from outlying communities taking refuge at the mission. Bead evidence helps us to glimpse how Guale people used newly available glass beads in ways both similar to and different from familiar shell beads, and how they repro-duced connections to their home communities in their patterned use of glass beads. The 1680 attack by the English and allies referred to above ended this mission venture. However, similar interactions were repeated over centuries, with glass beads often acting as a pivot point between extant systems of valuation and the novel ones that emerged through colonial entanglements.

As illustrated by examples throughout this chap-ter, small, often humble things participate in the making of social life in communities across the world and through time. Things act as resources in the making of personhood, identity, and community. They participate in creating and recalibrating value (what is esteemed, what is imbued with power). They are primary resources through which people think through and communicate their place in the world. In a nutshell, things matter in history and archaeology matters because it helps us to appreciate how they do so in practice, the topic to which we turn next.

4

Practice and Knowledge

So perhaps *how it comes to be* is really more distinctive of culture than what it *is*.

Alfred Kroeber, *Anthropology* (New York: Harcourt, Brace, 1948), p. 253 (emphasis original)

Culture is a word much used in media and in casual conversation today. It can describe something refined (like taste in art or music) or something widely shared (consumer culture). For much of the 20th century, it was associated with what anthropologists studied, but, by the turn of the millennium, this key notion escaped the ivory tower to become part of common vocabulary. The fact that a spike in look-ups prompted Merriam-Webster to declare "culture" its 2014 "word of the year"[1] tells us that, despite widespread use, we are not clear on what culture "is."

This matters because culture comes quickly to mind when we think of archaeology. For example, museums organize archaeological displays by "regional cultures" and portray time as a succession of named cultures. This reflects culture's role as a key notion in 20th-century archaeology and anthropology. Today, however, archaeologists and anthropologists are more likely to focus attention on social action or *practice* rather than culture. Understanding why culture figures less prominently in these fields today lays a foundation for considering alternatives. Therefore, let's take another quick dip into intellectual history before we do so.

Academic disciplines tend to be associated with key notions of what they study: for psychology, mind and cognition; for sociology, society; for economics, the economy. From the late 19th century, anthropology claimed culture as its focus and set about trying to define it. Generations of 20th-century anthropologists vigorously debated the fine points, giving rise to the adage that a roomful of 20 anthropologists would yield as many definitions. Nonetheless, common themes emerged and these in turn shaped archaeology, particularly in North America (where it is most often a sub-field of anthropology) and places where North American-trained archaeologists worked.

In one meaning, culture refers to a shared capacity among modern humans (*Homo sapiens sapiens*) to learn and transmit behaviors over generations. This capacity, founded in language, distinguishes humans from non-human animals. Archaeologists who study differences between modern humans and other hominins (like Neanderthals) talk about culture in this singular, *universal* sense, seeking evidence for when this capacity developed and its effects on the course of human history.

A second and more common meaning refers to the distinctive customs, values, and behaviors of a specific society. Again, emphasis is on what we learn, acquire, share, and transmit across generations, and, in this regard, some characterize culture as layered atop biology. Thought of in this (overly simplistic) way, we are born with biology, but become equipped with culture's learned inheritance as a member of a particular society. These learned ways account for the great variety in how people of different societies reckon family membership (kinship), celebrate life transitions (birth, marriage, death), build houses, make a living, and so on. People everywhere do all of these things, but the bundle of ways specific to a group is culture in the *particular* sense. Some early 20th-century anthropologists went further, describing culture as "super-organic," with the implication that it is something with a life of its own beyond individuals who "belong" to that culture.

In defining culture in this particular and plural sense (culture*s*), 20th-century anthropologists regularly used terms like norms, beliefs, values, modes of thought, traditions, customs, symbols, and ideals typical of a group. Recalling the commonsensical principles we touched on in Chapter 2, culture was often understood as springing from ideas, concepts, and the mind, with so-called "material culture" reflecting a culture's mental templates (Chapter 3). Seen through this "idealist" lens, archaeological materials helped to map the distribution and duration of individual cultures, but only at some remove from the ideas and beliefs seen as culture's primary source. The implication was that culture was an intangible and difficult "thing" for archaeologists to study.

Another mid-century view of culture seemed to offer greater promise for archaeologists. Influenced by materialist strands of thought, American anthropologist Leslie White described Culture (singular, proper noun) as "an extrasomatic [outside the body] tradition," the function of which is "the harnessing of energy and putting it to work in the service of man."[2] White saw technology as the interface that enabled "man" to overcome nature, a notion compatible with principles of western common sense that we touched on in Chapter 2. From the 1960s, many archaeologists embraced White's project of tracing the evolution of Culture by studying technology and its efficiency in getting food and capturing energy. All parties to these early debates wrote of culture in terms of layered domains: ideational, social, and material or technological. However, unlike those who stressed the formative role of ideas in shaping culture, those who followed White emphasized technology and material conditions as formative, about which more shortly.

From around the 1930s, archaeologists working in North America and Europe began to use culture as a shorthand to capture the similarities and differences among archaeological materials across space and through time. Though inspired to use the term by different sources on either side of the Atlantic,[3] cultures became classificatory building blocks of archaeological chronologies. By grouping sites with similar artifacts (e.g., distinctive pottery styles), archaeologists identified geographical clusters, known as culture areas. These clusters emphasized similarities within and difference between units, portrayed as bounded in space and time. When it came to understanding change over time, this focused attention on "transitions" between archaeological cultures. Despite the fact that early anthropologists like Alfred Kroeber acknowledged the importance of paying attention to how cultures come to be (see the opening quote in this chapter), scholars tended instead to emphasize their characteristic traits. By extension, individual cultures were assumed stable and persistent until they transformed into something new or were replaced (e.g., by the migration of new people).

Though early archaeologists defined these units based on material culture, the implication soon took hold that archaeological cultures – like the Mogollon or Hohokam in the American Southwest, or the Iron Age Hallstatt or La Tène cultures of Europe – reflected social units like language groups, tribes, chiefdoms, and so on. In world regions where the interface between so-called "history" and "prehistory" was recent (in other words, colonized areas), it seemed easy to assume that ethnographic cultures (those described by 19th- and 20th-century missionaries, colonial officials, and anthropologists) provided an analogical mirror for their "prehistoric" antecedents (Chapter 2). This fueled a belief that archaeology could contribute little to our understanding of recent centuries in these regions. In fact, as amply demonstrated by ongoing research across the globe, archaeology is a key source for learning about how people in the past navigated changing circumstances, including recent centuries of colonialism. As we saw in Chapter 3, careful study of archaeological materials helps us to appreciate how people through their daily practices participate in the making, reproduction, and transformation of values and traditions – in short, what we call culture – whether in ancient times or today.

A cartoon sketch of some of this earlier thinking about culture might portray it as a chest of scrolls inscribed with behavioral codes handed down through generations. In its super-organic guise, the chest hovers overhead. Elders initiate youth into the rules' intricacies: whom to marry, how to be a chief, how to properly celebrate a rite. The scrolls precede individual people and persist after they are gone. Conceived in this way, people have little agency, other than to reproduce culture by following its rules or codes. Transformation comes from outside forces – with warfare, migration, and climate change as key suspects. Tradition looms large in this way of thinking about culture, with change seen as diluting cultural "authenticity" and fueling judgements about how "real" members of a culture should behave.

This way of thinking about culture – and similarly what some social scientists call structure – does not mesh with lived experience. Of course, anyone who lives within the bounds of a modern nation state (i.e., everyone) is well familiar with structure and rules; they abound in schools, government, and other formal institutions. But both within and outside such institutions, much of what we know about how to act and do things does not come from rules or formal codes. Yes, we learn from our elders, but we do so more often through example or story than by explicit rules. Over time we glean from daily contexts what is appropriate and inappropriate: how to dress, what to eat, how to act in public compared to private spaces, how to use tools, and so on. We learn from things and the actions and responses of those around us. We develop a sensibility – what some call a cultural logic – of how to act through our interactions with people and things (Chapter 3).

This sensibility is more akin to guidelines – what some anthropologists call a disposition – than rules. In new situations, our internalized (embodied) sensibility provides a springboard for improvising and innovating. Viewed from this vantage point, culture is emergent: it springs from practice, which involves interaction with other people, beings, and things. Importantly, the continuity of what we call "tradition" is made through everyday actions, and traditions are continuously altered through practice in specific situations (the context of practice, who is present, in what conditions). The important upshot is that continuity through time is made through practice. So is change. Practice – people doing things – is a site of culture-making, and what we call "culture" is an extrapolation from practice. This applies equally to contexts governed by formal codes that may not be faithfully observed. In short, cultural forms take shape through histories of everyday practice.

Why do these debates about culture matter? Each of us – every day in every way – participates in making what we call "culture," albeit, as Marx said of history, not just as we please but under conditions shaped by prior and wider circumstance, including institutional constraints. If culture is not like a box of scrolls handed down through generations, but instead the emergent outcome of ongoing reproduction, negotiation, improvisation, and innovation, then culture is not a *thing* but a *process*. Processes are dynamic: they involve ongoing streams of action. We might freeze-frame action in order to map what is going on – to discern structure – but that analytical move fosters a sense that the map comes before action instead of emerging out of it. The same holds true for the thing we call "society": societies take shape through ongoing streams of daily practice, as do the key notions that we call class, gender, ethnicity, and other ways of distinguishing among people.

Why does this matter for archaeology? If past cultures, societies, and categories of people (like elites and commoners) were made, reproduced, and transformed through ongoing action, archaeology specializes in studying material traces of those actions. If, as we considered in Chapter 3, things are not just reflections of thought impressed on the world, but instead agents in forming our sensibilities and shaping daily practice, then the material traces of those things provide important evidence for past culture-making processes.

Another important implication: culture-making practices take form through intergenerational knowledge and knowhow. Yet the histories and connections of people who handed knowledge down through generations are poorly captured by 20th-century archaeology's time-space regional culture boxes. People in the past moved around, exchanged ideas and ways of doing things. They intermarried and otherwise interacted in ways obscured when we approach the past as if people lived in geographical containers. Similarly, the historically recent names that pigeon-hole people by nationality, ethnicity, or tribal affiliation mask the numerous connections, relationships, and circulations that crossed those boundaries. Many of these names are a product of recent colonial processes. Though they have shaped people's lives since, they can hobble rather than aid understanding of everyday action if we uncritically project them into earlier times (Chapter 2).

In short, studying the materiality of culture-making processes in times recent and ancient helps us to understand culture-making *in practice* – including how boundaries between social groups were made (and made porous) in the past and today. Thus, an archaeology focused on culture-making practices (a *process*) rather than culture (a *thing*) lends new perspective on the worlds we have inherited, the ones we make, and the ones we will bequeath to those who follow. It does so by using archaeological materials to study *genealogies* of practice, a key notion that refers to historical connections among specific ways of doing things (practices) and how they change through time.

Knowledge in Practice

Knowledge and knowhow are sources of continuity and change in practice. Scholars distinguish between *explicit* and *tacit* knowledge. Explicit knowledge is put into words ("Elbows off the table!" "Bow before your king!"), whether written or not. It can also be codified through non-linguist representation, as in the carved figures on Pacific Northwest coast house posts (so-called "totem poles"), which convey family histories and attest hereditary rights and privileges. Tacit knowledge is non-linguistic and comes through bodily engagement: how to manipulate a tool, how to balance on a bicycle, how it feels to transgress a social boundary of which you were unaware. Both are sources of what we call culture, but importantly neither exists independently of practice.

Knowledge is transferred within and between generations through learning, which can happen formally (think school) or informally (like learning to cook by helping those who prepare your food). Much learning takes place through routine practice (observing, imitating, trial and error). At first, learners (often children) do things that require little skill (in cooking: fetching, peeling, stirring). With time, they try their hand at new skills and become habituated in the ways of practice: techniques like how to hold and use a tool, how to handle clay while forming a pot. This involves tacit knowledge (like gestures and bodily habits) as well as explicit knowledge (like a dish's ingredients and their proportions). Through trial and error, learners become increasingly skilled in tasks (whether cooking, making a pot from clay, or forging metal from ore) and they move from the periphery to full integration in what scholars call a *community of practice*. Communities of practice include learners and doers who work together in face-to-face settings and share ways of doing (called practical repertoires). Because they are based in practice, these communities are sites both for reproducing customary ways of doing things and for changing them as their members improvise and innovate, which can happen as people become involved in wider networks of interaction, confront changes in resource availability, and engage in changing circumstances more generally.[4]

Archaeologists find community of practice to be a helpful alternative to the big bins of "culture" described above. Individuals learn how to do a variety of things across a range of contexts, forming their identities as they do so. Importantly, they can be members of multiple communities of practice. For example, potters who learn and practice their craft in a shared community might participate in different religious communities or speak different first languages. So too do some craftspeople participate in communities of practice wider in scope than their residential communities, visiting and learning from fellow craftspeople who live elsewhere. Networks of learning and sharing can lead to widespread ways of doing things – called *constellations of practice* – that encompass people who are distinguished from one another in other respects (belonging to different linguistic communities of practice, among other possibilities). In short, communities of practice can be like a Venn diagram – distinct but also overlapping – with people forming identities through their participation in more than one community of practice. Using archaeological materials to map these overlapping communities in space and through time looks very different from 20th-century ethnographic maps that portray neatly bounded tribes or ethnicities.

By studying the materiality (Chapter 3) of learning networks – how they are expressed in artifacts – archaeologists are able to develop new insights into the social dynamics of ancient societies. As a rapid example, women often learn to make pottery in their birth communities, after which they may marry out, taking up residence in their husband's community. Here they may experience pressure to make pots that conform to styles of their new localities. As they do so, they may continue to draw on tacit embodied knowledge (like gestures) from their earlier experience. How they prepare their clay, whether they build a pot by coiling or drawing clay up and out from a lump – these are aspects of a learned technological style that they may continue to practice even if they make differently shaped and decorated pots. Archaeologists working in the American Southwest, Africa, and Amazonia have used these kinds of clues to tease out the social networks expressed in technological styles of pottery and study how they varied geographically and through time.

Careful study of individual pots has also enabled archaeologists to develop insights into how past people taught and learned craft skills. Archaeologist Patricia Crown has studied thousands of painted pottery vessels spanning the period from 900 to 1450 CE from across the American Southwest. She can distinguish pots made by learners – most probably young girls – from those made by skilled potters. Learners' pots are asymmetrical, lumpy, poorly fired, and have clumsily painted designs. In other cases, a pot with a well-executed painted design on the interior may have a rough exterior design made with a finger rather than a fine brush, showing how learners and skilled potters worked collaboratively on individual pots (Figure 5). Careful study also

Figure 5. White Mountain Redware bowl (St. Johns Polychrome) showing forming and interior decoration by a skilled potter and exterior finger painted by a learning potter. Arizona State Museum Catalog Number GP01975. 16 cm in maximum width. Photograph by Marianne Tyndall, supplied courtesy of Patricia Crown.

shows how skilled potters created scaffolding for learners: painting well-executed lines to divide the pot's surface into sections and start a design, after which the apprentice completed it.[5] Both examples demonstrate direct adult involvement in children's learning during the past that differs from what ethnographers described for the region, where young girls were said to learn primarily by observing and imitating their female relatives.

Focusing on practice (a process) rather than culture (a thing) prompts new questions and new techniques for coaxing evidence from archaeological materials. As Crown's study shows, it helps us to gain perspective on a range of actors in the past: in this case (probably) adult women and girls. It can help us to understand how social boundaries were actively made (think sumptuary laws that governed who could wear or have certain things) and transgressed in specific times and places. A focus on practice tends to address "how" rather than "why" questions. By focusing attention on past practice – its continuities and changes – we develop valuable insight into how life came to be as it was in specific times and places. Where we have good chronological understanding of contexts, we can also gauge whether change happened gradually or rapidly.

Before highlighting examples of how archaeologists do this, let's return to the idea of culture as a cake made from ideational, social, and technological layers. We know from experience that life does not sort neatly in this way. An apparatus may be simultaneously a technological, social, and ideological thing (your cellphone is a close-at-hand example). Archaeologists have long been characterized as those who study culture's technological "layer," and this played well in relation to perspectives that stressed technology as the interface for human adaptation and driver of evolutionary progress. Yes, archaeologists study how people used technology to acquire and process resources, and, yes, we can chart the development of new tools, techniques, and their effects. But when we make practice and materiality a focus of study, we better appreciate interrelations between technology, social life, and our ways of both being in and thinking about our worlds.

Studying Practice

If practice refers to the actions of people in the world, how do we learn about people doing things from things found in the ground? In other words, how do move from studying things to studying processes?

First, archaeologists study processes at varying scales, from single events to long durations. The mummified remains of 5,300-year-old "Ötzi the Iceman," found by hikers in the Tyrolian Alps in 1991, yield clues to his last meal, his cause of death, his equipment, and his life history, among other details. His stomach contents held traces of his last meal, which included meat of wild animals (ibex and red deer) and einkorn wheat. A flint arrowhead embedded in his shoulder shows that he likely bled to death after the arrow pierced his artery. His well-preserved clothing was made of leather and fur, atop which he wore a cloak fashioned from grass. Though he consumed wild meat, some of his leather garments were made of domestic animal skins (sheep and cattle). Chemical analyses of these revealed a previously unknown tanning process, which experimental studies suggest lent superior water repellency.[6] Ötzi's mummified remains thus offer insight into action at scales ranging from an event (a meal) to intergenerational technical know-how (his copper axe and tanned hides).

Few archaeological finds lend themselves to such fine-grained understanding of events, whether a meal, an attack, or a window into the clothing and equipment used by an individual on a single day. The October CE 79 eruption of Mount Vesuvius created the iconic examples of point-in-time archaeological sites Pompeii and Herculaneum. Yet even these are not time capsules of life frozen in a moment. The towns were affected differently over the course of Vesuvius' eruption and people disturbed both sites by digging centuries before archaeologists worked there.[7]

What archaeologists confront more often when they expose settlements are houses and artifacts from different moments in time, even if they appear as part of the same contexts. A garbage heap contains the remains of many meals and things discarded over many months, years, or centuries. A house's walls may have been built at different times and houses across a settlement may have been constructed and occupied at different times. Thus, an excavated site might encompass the daily practices of one generation, ten generations, or fifty, depending on how long people lived there. The complexity increases when we are dealing with multiple sites and their landscapes. Associations (Chapter 1) can help us to work out temporal relationships between contexts. Doing so is part of both the art and science of archaeology.[8] Based on these, archaeologists have become adept at teasing out culture-making practices at varying time scales.

Consider mounds and earthworks. They appear as finished products that transform their surroundings. Some are settlement mounds built up as generations of people lived and rebuilt on the same site (think Near Eastern sites like Ancient Jericho, which are artificial mounds that archaeologists call "tells"). Others are deliberately constructed monumental earthworks, including the iconic UNESCO World Heritage sites of Cahokia Mounds and Poverty Point located along the Mississippi

River Valley corridor. Deliberately built mounds were a feature of ancient landscapes across eastern North America during what archaeologists call the Archaic, Woodland, and Mississippian periods, just as they were in the British Isles from the Neolithic to the Anglo-Saxon periods. Not coincidentally, these were times of social elaboration, and many earthworks are interpreted as places where rituals were performed, often on a seasonal basis, and visited, revisited, and modified, sometimes over centuries. Some were built rapidly, others incrementally, only gradually taking the form of the "finished products" mapped by archaeologists. Until recently, archaeologists focused more attention on their function than the processes through which these earthworks came to be. As recent research demonstrates, attention to mound-making processes lends valuable new insights into the ancient communities that built them.

New questions arise if we approach mounds as a process (how they came to be) rather than a thing (finished product). Building a mound involves more than just carrying baskets of dirt, piling them up, and tamping them down. It requires skills, know-how, planning, and coordination, not the least of which involves mobilizing labor and materials. The building process – which might span months or generations – was equally as important as activities focused on the mounds in their "finished" form.[9] Moreover, sites like Poverty Point and Cahokia comprised larger mound complexes that show spatial planning and evidence for spatial reworking over time.

Poverty Point is an extraordinary landscape engineered by Indigenous Americans during what archaeologists call the Late Archaic period (2000–500 BCE). Its monumental core (Figure 6) covers about 140 ha and includes five mounds of varying size and shape (conical, flat-topped, effigy-shaped) organized around a plaza enclosed by six semi-circular raised ridges of varying height (up to 2 m). Laid end-to-end, the ridges would run about 10 km in length, and estimates of the volume of earth moved in building the complex range from 750,000 to 1,000,000 m³. To lend perspective, Poverty Point's residents began building these earthworks about three centuries before Tutankhamun ruled Egypt. However, unlike the people of agricultural Egypt, those who built Poverty Point lived by hunting, collecting, and fishing.

For decades, archaeologists disbelieved that "hunter-gatherers" could have built a city-scale complex like Poverty Point. They assumed that such communities spent their days caught up in a

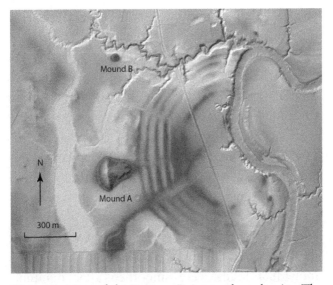

Figure 6. Map of the Poverty Point earthworks site. The earthworks are situated to the west of the meandering Bayou Macon. A Louisiana State Route (LA-577) bisects the site's plaza, which is enclosed by C-shaped ridges. Base map courtesy of Poverty Point Station Archaeology Program, University of Louisiana Monroe.

daily food quest and therefore lacked the necessary time, organization, and social coordination – a view shaped by ethnographic understandings of groups like the Kalahari San of southern Africa living in very different times and environments. But in an example that shows how archaeological evidence forces a rethink, recent research makes clear that people who lived by hunting, collecting, and fishing built this mound complex some 3,500 years ago.

Work conducted over decades (1950s through 2020s) has shed light on how Poverty Point's mounds and ridges were built, with implications for understanding practice at different scales. Early work focused on Mound B, where archaeologists saw evidence of several construction phases, each ending in flat surfaces and the last adding a conical cap to the mound. In some layers, archaeologists could distinguish loads of differently colored dirt, some still in the haystack form created when the dirt was tipped from its container. In other cases, individual loads were smoothed after dumping. Basketry impressions in the dirt provide clues to the containers used, though archaeologists suspect that hide bags were also employed. These traces suggest that containers held loads of dirt weighing about 50 lb. If accurate, Mound B alone required an estimated 278,800 basket loads of dirt. Mound A is even larger, measuring 215 × 200 m at the base and requiring upwards of 15.5 million loads – a volume equivalent to filling an American football field to a height of 45 m.[10]

Remarkably, given its size, recent work shows that Mound A was raised rapidly. Rainfall is high and frequent in the region, so an absence of eroded surfaces within mound layers implies that people built the mound in a span of months. Its lowest level was a thick layer of light-colored silt, mined and transported to the mound site, then laid atop dark clay-rich soil of an existing swale. Layers placed over the light level were darker. However, these layers are not simply "dirt." Close study of their constituent materials show that specific soils were selected – sometimes for texture, other times for color – and often transported over considerable distances. In short, the sediments are artifacts created by human choices. While archaeologists cannot know for sure the intentions behind these choices (which were surely multiple), they were clearly meaningful and deliberate. The implication is that many people came together to make this happen in a process that involved careful planning and coordination of an exceptional labor effort that was quite apparently *not* beyond the capacity of people who lived by hunting, collecting, and fishing.

Rather than treating mounds as backdrops to ritual activities that might have taken place atop or around them, studying mound-making processes asks how the building of them was part and parcel of ritualized social group-making processes. As they rose from the ground, mounds transformed surrounding landscapes, becoming a presence experienced by all who came within their orbits. But as many archaeologists argue today, the act of building also transformed people through a process of collective action, in this case probably oriented toward a larger cosmic purpose (such as re-enacting a creation story). Though we can only guess at these intentions, the society that flourished at Poverty Point for centuries took form through mound-building processes to which many people devoted much effort.

Gaining insight into how communities are made through activities like mound-building is but one example of the way in which a focus on practice helps us to understand how culture comes to be, to persist, and to change. Studying histories or genealogies of practice (histories of doing) matters because these lay the foundation for future actions. They are relevant to understanding processes through which communities and polities persist and how they fall apart or dissolve, a topic hotly debated under the headline-attracting term "collapse."

If collapse has an ancient poster child, it is Classic Mayan civilization. Over Classic period centuries (about 250–950 CE), kingdoms and city-states developed across the lowland Yucatán Peninsula and highland areas to the south. Ambitious construction projects resulted in iconic temple cities like

Tikal, Copán, and Calakmul – all today UNESCO World Heritage sites and tourist destinations – but other kingdoms and administrative centers emerged across the expansive and ecologically diverse area today known as southern Mexico, Guatemala, Honduras, Belize, and El Salvador. They shared a suite of practices and knowledge systems including writing, sophisticated calendric, astronomical, and mathematical knowledge, and, in later times, an institution of divine kingship.

In a region with little standing water and seasonal rainfall, technologies of water management and water-focused ritual were a primary concern for Mayan political-religious leaders and a source of their power. Communities built elaborate infrastructure to move and store seasonally available water, and ritual practice was central to ensuring its reliable availability. Varied water management practices and infrastructure across the region enabled Mayan kingdoms to develop and flourish in water-scarce regions, but not indefinitely.

Long-standing elements of Mayan political order unraveled across the Maya Lowlands during the Terminal Classic (about 850–950 CE). Cities were abandoned, albeit at different times and not universally so. Supporting populations detached themselves from royal courts and the principle of divine kingship dissolved. Scholars have vigorously debated potential causes: climate change, soil degradation, population pressure, warfare, invasion, disease. But an important takeaway from recent research is that apocalyptic collapse scenarios ignore the fact that the Maya did not disappear – over 7 million Mayan-speaking people live across the region today – and archaeological research centered on smaller settlements, minor centers, and the daily lives of the "99%" (ordinary people) tells a story other than collapse.[11]

Yes, many people left the temple cities. Yes, there was less investment in monumental building, and there is ample evidence that the divinity of rulers came into question, perhaps in the face of recurrent drought. However, depopulation in some areas saw gains in others. Centers proved fragile, but Mayans lived on and continued to reproduce their communities through familiar agricultural, landscape, and ritual practices, some in new locations and others continuing to live in the landscapes created by their forebears. The trajectories of specific cities and communities depended in part on the rigidity of practice – how fully leaders doubled down on the rituals that worked in the past but failed in the face of changing circumstance – alongside factors that tethered people to place, including long-lasting improvements to landscape inherited from previous generations, or what scholars term "landesque capital."[12] In short, how "collapse" played out varied considerably in relation to local circumstance and contexts of practice.

Archaeology provides a long lens on the fragility of polities, their alliances and networks, but importantly also on the variety of circumstances that contributed to their dissolution and its effects on daily life. The long view often underscores "resiliency" – a contemporary buzzword in the academy and media – in the face of eventful times. Overcoming hardship and coping are implied in the word, and resiliency is founded in the knowledge systems and improvisational practices that give form to our daily lives. Culture can serve as a shorthand reference for these. But as a subject focused on the materiality of practice in times ancient and recent, archaeology matters because it lends perspective on culture-making as a dynamic process through which communities and wider constellations of practice are made. In short, it helps us see how the wider world of which we are part and which our children and grandchildren will inherit takes form.

5

Possibilities

The narratives we create become the reality we expect.

Chris Begley, *The Next Apocalypse: The Art and Science of Survival* (New York: Basic Books, 2021), p. 95

Before turning to how archaeology lends perspective on today and the future, let's recap some points about why archaeology matters.

First, archaeological materials are a primary source for learning about 99 percent of human history for which we have no textual evidence. They also lend insight into daily lives during the 1 percent of history "covered" by texts. They reveal what people did – as compared to said – and bring to view the lives of those invisible in textual sources. Archaeology helps us to understand how past communities engaged with one another and their surroundings, deepening our appreciation of whence we came and how our worlds took form and changed. How we go about studying those histories matters, as do archaeologists' relationships with contemporary communities who claim them.

Second, analogy – a logical process through which we relate the unfamiliar to the familiar – is central to how we develop insight into past times using archaeological materials. How we wield the tool is critical. Analogies supply hypotheses that we comparatively assess against an array of evidence. Lack of fit is as informative as fit. It tells us how life in the past differed from recent times, pressing us to ask new questions and cast our interpretive net wider. An important source for doing so is to look beyond the tenets of western "common sense" and respectfully engage with non-European ways of being and knowing as sources that enlarge possibilities. They encourage attention to how humans shape their worlds through relations with other living and non-living beings and things, forming landscapes and making places through long histories of interaction. By enlarging possibilities for understanding the past, archaeology matters because it also expands our perspective on today and the future.

Third, we enrich understanding when we pay attention to things and materials as active elements of lifeways. Things and technologies participate in how we relate to one another and our surroundings. We make social commonalities and differences through things. Things shape and reform the values through which generations make themselves and navigate change. They matter in history because things matter in human lives. History told without them lacks depth. Archaeology brings this depth to human history while helping us to appreciate how things, materials, and technologies configure world-making practices today.

Fourth, archaeology reveals how people create intergenerational relations, communities, and wider social constellations through practice. Culture may serve as a useful shorthand for the distinctive conventions of specific communities, but it conceals more than it reveals about how those conventions emerge, endure, and change. Focusing instead on practice reminds us that culture- and place-making are processes, never fixed-and-finished and equally ongoing in times of change and continuity. A focus on practice helps us to understand how people in the past drew on their knowledge systems to respond to shifting circumstances like climate change, expanding social networks, and newly available resources. In doing so, archaeology lends perspective on how we make our communities and wider worlds *in practice* today.

In short, archaeology matters because it enlarges our understanding of and ways of thinking about human histories. By expanding our narratives of whence we came, it helps us to appreciate how present-day circumstances bear the imprint of past practice and encourages us to think anew about present-day and future realities and possibilities. Let's consider examples of how.

Archaeology helps us to understand the millennial-scale processes through which people interacted with plants, animals, and things to produce landscapes and shows how Indigenous practices of resource management – including low-impact farming – sustained and enhanced vital resources (Chapter 2). An important implication for today is that we should stop imagining Nature as a thing untouched by humans until recently. Archaeological evidence shows that biodiversity has a history in which humans played a part, pushing us to rethink strategies of conservation biology or restoration ecology modeled on notions of Nature without humans. As an example, US Forest Service officials in California are engaging with archaeologists and Indigenous knowledge keepers of the Amun Mutsun Band to learn about ancestral practices of controlled burning as a source of new possibilities for managing the intensifying wildfires that currently threaten us.[1]

As in the past, circulations and entanglements with things shape our lives today. An emerging focus on "contemporary archaeology" or "archaeology without antiquity" shows us how they do so.[2] These studies approach times from the 20th century as an archaeological period distinctive for how much stuff we consume, for how much rubbish we generate, and for landscape and biosphere transformations that affect the sustainability of life. As one example, recall how archaeologists apply sourcing and contextual analysis to study the itineraries of glass beads (Chapter 3). Archaeologists use similar methods to study plastic waste washing ashore on remote Pacific islands, ending up in the stomachs of sea creatures or swirling in a Great Pacific Garbage Patch. Tracing the itineraries of discarded single-use plastics back to their use source helps to foster changing practice as people come to appreciate the unintended consequences of daily actions.[3]

Archaeology helps us to appreciate how today's taken-for-granted arrangements – ones we treat as natural – came about through past action. Archaeological studies of colonialism – ancient and recent – provide a wealth of examples.[4] Colonizers and colonized people alike made themselves anew through materials and things that flowed through intercontinental networks, albeit not under conditions in which everyone was free to choose. Archaeologists shed light on how these flows changed value systems and participated in new ways of making and maintaining social categories and boundaries, including gender, ethnicity, race, and nationality. By demonstrating the "made" character of these arrangements and historicizing them, archaeology supports possibilities for understanding how, through small things and daily practice, we make forms of similarity and difference today. Understanding these as made rather than given opens possibilities for making them differently – and more equitably – in future.

Archaeology demonstrates that the world has long been cosmopolitan, with things, people, plants, and animals moving across regions and continents. Though we treat globalization as a recent phenomenon, archaeology shows that intra- and intercontinental circulations of people and things have deep histories that gave rise to the world as we experience it. Though pandemic-related shutdowns and the war in Ukraine may have made "global supply chains" a topic of household conversation, archaeology shows how circulating things – commercial and otherwise – have long been taken up, been put to local uses, and shaped people's sense of self and others, as we saw in the case of Iron Age Europe or during Classic Yorùbá times (Chapter 3). Understanding these past processes helps us to analyze and understand the ongoing ways in which things and place-making participate in the shaping, maintaining, and challenging of social categories and boundaries today.

Archaeologists have long studied the headline-making issues that confront us today: climate change, disease, agricultural sustainability, biodiversity, waste disposal and pollution, population growth, migration, globalization, urban expansion, inequality, violence and warfare, social justice, and more. All these processes occurred in the past: sea levels rose and coastal cities were swamped; excessive rainfall and drought caused people to move and to adjust their economic activities; people's life chances were shaped by excessive inequality and conflict. The question that arises is: how applicable are archaeological insights to contemporary expressions of these social, political economic, and environmental problems? How useful is archaeological knowledge in addressing today's pressing issues?

Any answer needs to grapple with scalar differences between challenges in the past and in the present. Analysts use shorthand terms like the Anthropocene, the Great Acceleration, and the

Great Divergence for these. Scholars debate the tipping points. Yet there is general agreement that, from at least the start of the Industrial Age in the early 1800s, human action has accelerated Earth's ecological, geological, and chemical systems, contributing to a new Anthropocene epoch in which our actions affect climate change. The Great Acceleration refers to dramatic increases in consumption, production, and their cascading effects since World War II. The Great Divergence signals the widening gap between haves and have-nots, initially conceived as differences between rich and poor nations but increasingly seen in wealth inequalities across individuals and groups. Each of these phenomena has precedents in human history, but their naming underscores the marked scalar increases during recent times.

In light of these scalar differences, we should not think of lessons learned through archaeology as providing cookie-cutter solutions to present and future dilemmas. But archaeology does suggest useful principles to guide thinking as we grapple with ongoing and shared dilemmas. So too does it enrich our perspectives by providing past analogues arrived at through detailed studies of archaeological materials that cast present and future situations in new relief. Let's briefly consider these in turn.

Today's societies tend to value short-term over long-term thinking and action. Archaeology's long lens helps us to lift our heads and appreciate that the long term matters. Take the example of Classic Mayan civilization (Chapter 4). Through decades of detailed archaeological research, we have learned much about the interconnected social and environmental dynamics through which this civilization took form and endured for centuries. These many centuries saw short-term periods of stability punctuated by pulses of change. Archaeologists have developed rich insights into the processes and daily practices that shaped these trajectories, as well as their longer-term outcomes (what happened "in the end"). Like Monday morning quarterbacks who gather to discuss how Sunday's game *could* have been won, an archaeologist's view is retrospective. As meteorologists and economic analysts well know, using retrospective knowledge to predict future outcomes is less assured. Forecasting is a tricky business, and particularly so for archaeology in light of the scalar differences already mentioned.

While archaeology may not help us to augur future outcomes, it does provide wisdom that can benefit today's policy and planning. As demonstrated repeatedly by archaeological research across areas of the world, local context, variability, and contingency matter. Returning to the Mayan example, archaeology provides evidence for a shared constellation of practices that typified the Classic Maya. However, variation – in environmental setting, infrastructure, landscape and resource management practices – shaped how specific communities responded to challenges like drought. Long-term resiliency was place-based and shaped by the rigidity or flexibility of local infrastructure and the extent to which generations of investment in landscape practices enabled communities to reproduce themselves in place after temple cities fell from prominence. In short, archaeology underscores that cities and states come and go, but the resiliency of their constituent people is context-dependent.

Archaeology helps us to appreciate that what we today call resiliency – the ability to respond to changing circumstance – is enhanced by diversity. Archaeological research underscores that resiliency is grounded in communities of practice and their intergenerational knowledge systems. This applies whether the focus is on resources (like animals or plants), strategies (like ways of cultivating resources), technologies, or other phenomena. Archaeology tells us that societies characterized by a diversity of practices and knowledge systems demonstrate greater flexibility in the face of shifting circumstances (like climate change or resource availability) compared to those that lack diversity.

Histories of technologies show us over and over again how wider connections and exposure to alternative ways of doing things contribute to experimentation and transform practice. Europe's sea-faring "Age of Discovery" (1400–1600 CE) depended upon applications of technologies developed in China (the magnetic compass), the Arab Mediterranean (the lateen sail), and modifications to Byzantine astrolabes that facilitated astronomical navigation. Circulations of new plant foods made available through Columbian exchange remade dietary practices across the world, with much of the "Old World" coming to depend upon staples from the "New World" (maize, manioc, and potatoes) and vice versa (rice, wheat). These crops expanded alternatives or enabled people to respond to changing conditions like decreased access to fertile land (as experienced by Irish tenant farmers under English colonization). But as the mid-19th-century Irish Potato Famine made clear, when taken up as replacements for rather than additions to familiar cultigens, new crops had the effect of reducing food security. Archaeology sheds light on trajectories of agricultural experimentation and their contexts, as archaeologist Amanda Logan demonstrated in her study of diminishing food security over recent centuries in the Banda area of Ghana.[5] Studies like hers show how food insecurity came about through these wider entanglements and underscore that the sustainability of innovated practices is historically contingent. They remind today's policy makers that sustainability is a dynamic process that depends on resource diversity and flexible models rather than one-size-fits-all solutions.

In like fashion, archaeological studies of ancient urbanism widen the pool of models from which to imagine new urban ecologies in a time of climate change and rising sea levels. A shared feature of long-lived ancient urban centers in the semi-tropics and tropics was their low-density pattern. Urban neighborhoods were interspersed with small-scale gardens and agricultural supports (including water supplies) to create extensive agro-urban landscapes. These supported large populations: for example, Angkor in Cambodia is estimated to have had a population of 750,000 by 1100–1200 CE. Models such as these can prompt reflection on taken-for-granted premises, like densification as an imperative that drives much contemporary urban planning. Archaeological models provide food for thought on how to reimagine urban spaces as places built to ensure landscape durability and resilience while delivering the social advantages of urban centers.[6]

Archaeology also tempers the imaginative scenarios of post-apocalyptic life that are fodder for popular media. Chris Begley, an archaeologist and wilderness survival skills instructor, sets out in *The Next Apocalypse* (cited at the start of this chapter) why archaeology does not support fantasies of people surviving "collapse" through rugged, heroic individualism. He uses evidence-based case studies like the Classic Maya (Chapter 4) to argue that proximate causes of collapse are hard to identify as they happen (and equally hard to pin-point retrospectively) and that what we call collapse is a protracted rather than rapid process. How it plays out depends on our practices and the systems they give rise to – their flexibility, and how invested people are in maintaining them. We survive calamity as communities, not as isolated individuals or families. Rebuilding society depends upon a variety of skills, competencies, and forms of knowledge, as well as the ability to improvise and innovate as part of ongoing communities of practice.

These are but a few examples of how insights from archaeology can effectively move the needle on how we imagine possibilities for today and the future. In doing so, archaeology provides past analogues for future possibilities. This involves the logic outlined in Chapter 2, but now using analogues drawn from our understandings of the past prised open through archaeological sources. Recall that archaeologists began studies of ancient agriculture or urbanism through the lens of the familiar (recent forms of practice). Systematic study of archaeological evidence from around the world subsequently revealed widely varied practices and forms of ancient agriculture, landscape practices, and urbanism not found in recent practice. Understanding of these past forms has been expanded in turn by considering the premises and priorities of other ways of knowing (epistemology) and being (ontology). None will provide a one-size-fits-all solution to contemporary problem solving, but each provides a newfound "familiar" through which to imagine future possibilities.

As a tool for thinking about today and the future, archaeology's long-term perspective cultivates humility and tempers hubris. It helps us to recognize that life on earth changes, that strategies effective in the short term (centuries) can prove ineffective over the long run (many centuries and indeed millennia), and that context and historical contingency matter. Archaeology reminds us that actions have unintended consequences as they ripple across space and through time. When undertaken in partnership with communities who are deeply rooted in the landscapes their ancestors helped to create, archaeology helps us to appreciate that "wisdom sits in places."[7] Archaeological materials are powerful connectors to knowledge systems and lifeways of earlier times. By working collaboratively with descendant communities, archaeologists aid knowledge revitalization and the vital project of connecting youth to the place-based wisdom of their ancestors.[8] So too is archaeology vitalized by the inclusion of practitioners who expand archaeology's "we" beyond the narrow ranks of earlier decades.

This brings us to the role of archaeology in education. As an integrative subject that crosscuts the sciences, social sciences, humanities, and arts, archaeology holds expansive potential to enrich school- and community-based learning. This holds true for developing skills and enriching content. Archaeology encourages skills relevant to a variety of pursuits: observation, measurement, numeracy, inference, and problem solving; cultural literacy, story-telling, and empathetic imaginative engagement. It therefore contributes to integrative STEM (Science, Technology, Engineering, Math) and humanities/arts learning. Whether as a classroom subject or source of classroom examples, archaeology has the advantage of developing and honing skills through problems and materials that fascinate. It offers many opportunities for hands-on and active learning,[9] at the same time as it requires archaeologists to engage with educators and communities to develop useable learning resources. Working in collaboration with community members, librarians, and educators, my focus in recent years has shifted from digging to developing heritage-learning resources based on what we have learned through four decades of archaeological research about the dynamism of village life in West Africa over the last 1,000 years.[10] As such, I can attest that this is an exciting growth area for archaeology today and in the future.

Archaeology reminds us that the ground beneath our feet and the landscapes around us carry traces of those who came before. Expand your world by embracing opportunities to learn through archaeology about the people who shaped the places where you live and to which you travel. Draw on insights from archaeology to gain a new perspective on the material practices through which we make communities and places today. Let archaeology remind you of the long-standing connections across world regions that shaped our shared histories while people developed place-based solutions to common human challenges. Monuments may inspire awe, but always recall the small things forgotten that participate in the making of our worlds and the ones we bequeath to our children. Archaeology offers knowledge on how we got where we are and food for thought on where we imagine ourselves going.

Notes

Chapter 1 Archaeological Perspectives

1 Sonia Harmand et al., "3.3-Million-Year-Old Stone Tools from Lomekwi 3, West Turkana, Kenya," *Nature* 521 (2015).

2 Roger C. Echo-Hawk, "Ancient History in the New World: Integrating Oral Traditions and the Archaeological Record in Deep Time," *American Antiquity* 65 (2000). Also Akinwumi Ogundiran, *The Yorùbá: A New History* (Bloomington: Indiana University Press, 2020).

3 Bruce G. Trigger, "Alternative Archaeologies: Nationalist, Colonialist, Imperialist," *Man* (n.s.) 19 (1984).

4 For example, Joe Watkins, *Indigenous Archaeology: American Indian Values and Scientific Practice* (Walnut Creek, CA: AltaMira Press, 2000); Christina Luke and Morag Kersel, *US Cultural Diplomacy and Archaeology: Soft Power, Hard Heritage* (New York: Routledge, 2012).

5 Sangita Chari and Jaime M.N. Lavallee, eds., *Accomplishing NAGPRA* (Corvallis: Oregon State University Press, 2013). Also Sonya Atalay, *Community-based Archaeology: Research with, by and for Indigenous and Local Communities* (Berkeley: University of California Press, 2012).

6 See Peter Der Manuelian, *Digital Giza: Visualizing the Pyramids* (Cambridge, MA: Harvard University Press, 2017) for digital archiving of George Reisner's records on Giza and related sites. Visit digital Giza at *http://giza.fas.harvard.edu/*.

7 "An Overview of the Grey Friars Project," *https://le.ac.uk/richard-iii/grey-friars*.

8 On Canada's Truth and Reconciliation process, see *https://nctr.ca/records/reports/#trc-reports*. On using GPR in culturally sensitive ways, see William T.D. Wadsworth et al., "Integrating Remote Sensing and Indigenous Archaeology to Locate Unmarked Graves: A Case Study from Northern Alberta, Canada," *Advances in Archaeological Practice* 9 (2021).

9 R.H. Bewley et al., "New Light on an Ancient Landscape: Lidar Survey in the Stonehenge World Heritage Site," *Antiquity* 79 (2005).

10 On how satellite imagery is changing archaeological practice, see Sarah Parcak, *Archaeology from Space: How the Future Shapes our Past* (New York: Henry Holt and Company, 2019). On LiDAR at Angkor, Damian Evans, "Airborne Laser Scanning as a Method for Exploring Long-term Socio-ecological Dynamics in Cambodia," *Journal of Archaeological Science* 74 (2016).

11 Norman Yoffee, ed., *The Evolution of Fragility: Setting the Terms* (Cambridge: McDonald Institute for Archaeological Research, 2019). On ancient states, Norman Yoffee, *Myths of the Archaic State: Evolution of the Earliest Cities, States, and Civilizations* (Cambridge: Cambridge University Press, 2004).

12 Alison Wylie, *Thinking from Things: Essays in the Philosophy of Archaeology* (Berkeley: University of California Press, 2002).

Chapter 2 Time and Knowing

1 Matthew R. Goodrum, "Questioning Thunderstones and Arrowheads: The Problem of Recognizing and Interpreting Stone Artifacts in the Seventeenth Century," *Early Science and Medicine* 13 (2008). On the founding of archaeology as a subject, Bruce G. Trigger, *A History of Archaeological Thought*, second edition (Cambridge: Cambridge University Press, 2006).

2 Johannes Fabian, *Time and the Other: How Anthropology Makes Its Object* (New York: Columbia University Press, 1983).

3 Rooted in classical philosophy, the idea of a hierarchical Great Chain of Being combined with Christian thought during the Middle Ages. Position in the Chain was thought to stem from the original Creation. Enlightenment scholars argued that societies could move up the hierarchy, introducing the notion of progress as a mechanism of "improvement."

Nineteenth-century social evolutionists built on these ideas to argue that progress through stages of savagery, barbarism, and civilization was a universal social evolutionary process. See Arthur O. Lovejoy, *The Great Chain of Being: A Study of the History of an Idea* (Cambridge, MA: Harvard University Press, 1936); George W. Stocking, Jr., *Victorian Anthropology* (New York: Free Press, 1987); Michel-Rolph Trouillot, "Anthropology and the Savage Slot: The Poetics and Politics of Otherness," in his *Global Transformations* (New York: Palgrave Macmillan, 2003).

4 For an ambitious rewriting that draws on archaeology, see David Graeber and David Wengrow, *The Dawn of Everything: A New History of Humanity* (Toronto: McClelland & Stewart, 2021).

5 J.D. Lewis-Williams, "The Evolution of Theory, Method and Technique in Southern African Rock Art Research," *Journal of Archaeological Method and Theory* 13 (2006).

6 Robert Losey, "Animism as a Means of Exploring Archaeological Fishing Structures on Willapa Bay, Washington, USA," *Cambridge Archaeological Journal* 20 (2010).

7 See Chapter 1, note 12.

8 While scholars' estimates differ, there is wide agreement that Indigenous American communities suffered devastating population declines in the centuries following European colonization. For background on the Americas before and after Columbus, see Charles C. Mann, *1491: New Revelations of the Americas*

before Columbus and *1493: Uncovering the New World Columbus Created* (New York: Alfred A. Knopf, 2005 and 2011, respectively).

9 William Balée, *Cultural Forests of the Amazon: A Historical Ecology of People and Their Landscapes* (Tuscaloosa: University of Alabama Press, 2013).

10 William M. Denevan, *Cultivated Landscapes of Native Amazonia and the Andes* (New York: Oxford University Press, 2001).

11 See Manuel Arroyo-Kalin, "Landscaping, Landscape Legacies, and Amazonia," in Christian Isendahl and Daryl Stump, eds., *The Oxford Handbook of Historical Ecology and Applied Archaeology* (Oxford: Oxford University Press, 2019).

12 On Indigenous landscape management in the Pacific Northwest, see the Clam Garden Network (*https://clamgarden.com/*), a consortium of First Nations and academic researchers dedicated to disseminating knowledge about Indigenous mariculture, with implications for contemporary food security.

13 See Melinda A. Zeder, "Pathways to Animal Domestication," in Paul Gepts et al., eds., *Biodiversity in Agriculture: Domestication, Evolution, and Sustainability* (Cambridge: Cambridge University Press, 2012).

Chapter 3 Connections through Things

1 Dan Hicks, "The Material-Cultural Turn: Event and Effect," in Dan Hicks and Mary C. Beaudry, eds.,

The Oxford Handbook of Material Culture Studies (Oxford: Oxford University Press, 2010).

2 John Robb, "What Do Things Want? Object Design as a Middle Range Theory of Material Culture," in Lisa Overholtzer and Cynthia Robin, eds., *The Materiality of Everyday Life* (Archeological Papers of the American Anthropological Association, Number 26, 2015).

3 See Lynn Ceci, "The Value of Wampum among the New York Iroquois: A Case Study in Artifact Analysis," *Journal of Anthropological Research* 38 (1982). On repatriation, see Margaret M. Bruchac, "Broken Chains of Custody: Possessing, Dispossessing, and Repossessing Lost Wampum Belts," *Proceedings of the American Philosophical Society* 162 (2018).

4 Peter Wells, *How Ancient Europeans Saw the World: Vision, Patterns, and the Shaping of the Mind in Prehistoric Times* (Princeton, NJ: Princeton University Press, 2012), p. 65.

5 Ibid., p. 199.

6 Steven L. Kuhn and Mary C. Stiner, "Paleolithic Ornaments: Implications for Cognition, Demography and Identity," *Diogenes* 54 (2007).

7 Eric Trinkaus and Alexandra P. Buzhilova, "Diversity and Differential Disposal of the Dead at Sunghir," *Antiquity* 92, 361 (2018).

8 For a compelling overview of how Atlantic trade fueled new forms of production and consumption, see Sidney W. Mintz, *Sweetness and Power: The Place of Sugar in Modern History* (New York: Viking, 1985).

9 Akinwumi Ogundiran, *The Yorùbá: A New History* (Bloomington: Indiana University Press, 2020). For evidence on glass-making, see Abidemi Babatunde Babaloa et al., "Ile-Ife and Igbo Olokun in the History of Glass in West Africa," *Antiquity* 91, 357 (2017).

10 Ogundiran, *The Yorùbá*, p. 103.

11 For example, see Jeremy Prestholdt, *Domesticating the World: African Consumerism and the Genealogies of Globalization* (Berkeley: University of California Press, 2008).

12 Chris Gosden, *Archaeology and Colonialism: Cultural Contact from 5000 BC to the Present* (Cambridge: Cambridge University Press, 2004), p. 25.

13 David Hurst Thomas, *St. Catherines: An Island in Time* (Athens: University of Georgia Press, 2011).

14 Elliot H. Blair, "Glass Beads and Constellations of Practice," in Andrew P. Roddick and Ann B. Stahl, eds., *Knowledge in Motion: Constellations of Learning across Time and Place*, (Tucson: University of Arizona Press, 2016).

Chapter 4 Practice and Knowledge

1 *https://www.merriam-webster.com/words-at-play/2014-word-of-the-year/culture*.

2 Leslie A. White, *The Evolution of Culture: The Development of Civilization to the Fall of Rome* (Walnut Creek, CA: Left Coast Press, 2007; orig. 1959), p. 39.

3 See Bruce Trigger, *Time and Traditions: Essays in Archaeological Interpretation* (Edinburgh: Edinburgh University Press, 1978).

4 Jean Lave and Etienne Wenger, *Situated Learning: Legitimate Peripheral Participation* (Cambridge: Cambridge University Press, 1991). Also Etienne Wenger, *Communities of Practice: Learning, Meaning, and Identity* (Cambridge: Cambridge University Press, 1998).

5 Patricia Crown, "Learning and Teaching in the Prehispanic American Southwest," in Kathryn Kamp, ed., *Children in the Prehistoric Puebloan Southwest* (Salt Lake City: University of Utah Press, 2002).

6 Housed at the South Tyrol Museum of Archaeology in Bolzano, Italy (*https://www.iceman.it/en/the-iceman/*), the mummy is a focus of ongoing studies using new analytical techniques. For example, Alois G. Püntener and Serge Moss, "Ötzi, the Iceman and his Leather Clothes," *CHIMIA International Journal for Chemistry* 64 (2010).

7 Alison E. Cooley and M.G.L. Cooley, *Destruction of Pompeii and Herculaneum*, second edition (London: Routledge, 2013).

8 See Gavin Lucas, *Making Time: The Archaeology of Time Revisited* (New York: Routledge, 2021); and *Understanding the Archaeological Record* (Cambridge: Cambridge University Press, 2012). Also Michael B. Schiffer, *Formation Processes of the Archaeological Record* (Albuquerque: University of New Mexico Press, 1987).

9 Tristam R. Kidder and Sarah C. Sherwood, "Mound Building as Daily Practice," in Sarah E. Price and Philip J. Carr, eds., *Investigating the Ordinary: Everyday Matters in Southeast Archaeology* (Gainesville: Florida Scholarship Online, 2018); and "Look to the Earth: The Search for Ritual in the Context of Mound Construction," *Journal of Archaeological and Anthropological Sciences* 9 (2017). Also Tristam R. Kidder et al., "Multimethod Geoarchaeological Analyses Demonstrates Exceptionally Rapid Construction of Ridge West 3 at Poverty Point," *Southeastern Archaeology* 40 (2021).

10 Jenny Ellerbe and Diana M. Greenlee, *Poverty Point: Revealing the Forgotten City* (Baton Rouge: Louisiana State University Press, 2015).

11 Jeremy A. Sabloff, "How Maya Archaeologists Discovered the 99% through the Study of Settlement Patterns," *Annual Review of Anthropology* 48 (2019); Cynthia Robin, *Everyday Life Matters: Maya Farmers at Chan* (Gainesville: University of Florida Press, 2013).

12 Patricia A. McAnany et al., "Leaving Classic Maya Cities: Agent-Based Modeling and the Dynamics of Diaspora," in Geoff Emberling, ed., *Social Theory in Archaeology and Ancient History: The Present and Future of Counternarratives* (Cambridge: Cambridge University Press, 2016). Also studies in Maxime Lamoureux-St-Hilaire and Scott Macrae, eds., *Detachment from Place: Beyond an Archaeology of Settlement Abandonment* (Louisville: University of

Colorado Press, 2020); Lisa J. Lucero, *Water and Ritual: The Rise and Fall of Classic Maya Rulers* (Austin: University of Texas Press, 2006).

Chapter 5 Possibilities

1 Kara Manke, "Fighting Fire with Fire: A Q&A with Kent Lightfoot," Berkeley News, *https://news. berkeley.edu/2018/09/24/fighting-fire-with-fire-a-qa- with-kent-lightfoot/*. Also R.Q. Cuthrell et al., "A Land of Fire: Anthropogenic Burning on the Central Coast of California," in Terry L. Jones and Jennifer E. Perry, eds., *Contemporary Issues in California Archaeology* (Walnut Creek, CA: Left Coast Press, 2012).

2 Assaf Nativ and Gavin Lucas, "Archaeology without Antiquity," *Antiquity* 94, 376 (2020).

3 John Schofield et al., "Contemporary Archaeology as a Framework for Investigating the Impact of Disposable Plastic Bags on Environmental Pollution in Galápagos," *Journal of Contemporary Archaeology* 7 (2020).

4 Michael Dietler, *Archaeologies of Colonialism: Consumption, Entanglement, and Violence in Ancient Mediterranean France* (Berkeley: University of California Press, 2010).

5 Amanda Logan, *The Scarcity Slot: Excavating Histories of Food Security in Ghana* (Berkeley: University of California Press, 2020). Also Chelsea Fisher, "Archaeology for Sustainable Agriculture," *Journal of Archaeological Research* 28 (2020).

6 See Vernon L. Scarborough and Christian Isendahl, "Distributed Urban Network Systems in the Tropical Archaeological Record: Toward a Model for Urban Sustainability in the Era of Climate Change," *The Anthropocene Review* 7 (2020).

7 Keith H. Basso, *Wisdom Sits in Places. Landscape and Language Among the Western Apache* (Albuquerque: University of New Mexico Press, 1996).

8 The Pacific Northwest offers examples of how archaeology participates in the vitalization of place-based knowledge. See "Sq'éwlets: A Stó:lō-Coast Salish Community in the Fraser River Valley," *http://www.digitalsqewlets.ca/index-eng.php*; Rhoda Foster and Dale R. Croes, "Joint Tribal/College West Site Investigations: A Critical Need for Native Expertise," *Journal of Wetland Archaeology* 4 (2004). See also Patricia A. McAnany, *Mayan Cultural Heritage: How Archaeologists and Indigenous Communities Engage the Past* (Lanham, MD: Rowman & Littlefield, 2016).

9 For example, learning resources available through the non-profit Project Archaeology based at Montana State University, *https://projectarchaeology.org/*.

10 "Banda through Time," hosted by the University of Victoria Libraries, *https://exhibits.library.uvic.ca/spotlight/iaff*.

Further Reading

It is challenging to winnow the many engaging and wide-ranging accounts of archaeology to a short list of suggested readings. In what follows, I highlight accounts of how archaeologists go about studying things, how they do fieldwork and use evidence to work through controversies. A second group of readings uses archaeological evidence to explore topics of contemporary concern (biodiversity, climate change, urban collapse, managing water), with each work offering perspective on present-day issues. A third group highlights engaging accounts of iconic sites and points readers to series that provide authoritative summaries of archaeology on world regions and topical issues. The list concludes with a forum on career possibilities published by the Society for American Archaeology.

Further Reading

Studying Things and Doing Fieldwork

Mary Beaudry, *Findings: The Material Culture of Needlework and Sewing* (New Haven, CT: Yale University Press, 2006).

Among the many objects that archaeologists recover during excavations are things classified as "small finds." Unlike common finds such as pottery, stone tools, or animal bones, small finds are often personal objects associated with the identities of those who owned or used them. In this book, historical archaeologist Mary Beaudry focuses attention on the small finds associated with needlework and sewing, exploring what they tell us about the lives of the women and men who used them. Beaudry describes how, after years of recovering simple pins, needles, thimbles, and other sewing paraphernalia, she undertook more systematic inquiry to understand their varied meanings in relation to their contexts of use in times ranging from the Neolithic to recent centuries. In doing so, she models how archaeologists use humble, everyday objects to develop substantive insights into unrecorded everyday lives of people.

Steve Brown, Anne Clarke, and Ursula Frederick, eds., *Object Stories: Artifacts and Archaeologists* (Walnut Creek, CA: Left Coast Press, 2015).

Archaeologists tells stories about the past through objects. Over recent decades, many archaeologists have experimented with new ways of writing that personalize the past: developing stories told from the perspective of the people who made or used the things that archaeologists unearth from the ground. This edited collection brings together archaeologists who work in different regions and periods to tell stories through objects. The volume opens with a chapter reprinted from Janet D. Spector's innovative *What This Awl Means: Feminist Archaeology at a Wahpeto Dakota Village* (St. Paul: Minnesota Historical Society Press, 1993), which inspired the collection. The book's chapters include stories of objects ranging from a million-year-old Acheulian hand axe to a tin door fashioned from USAID tin cans in early 21st-century Uganda. The 25 object essays combine impressions of how archaeologists are affected by the things they find with explorations of the imaginative potential that evocative artifacts inspire.

Alice Beck Kehoe, *Controversies in Archaeology* (Walnut Creek, CA: Left Coast Press, 2008).

Archaeology is often drawn into popular debates about the past, some fueled by sci-fi fantasies like the role of extraterrestrials in founding ancient civilizations. Other controversies are more grounded in realistic alternatives, like the extent to which ancient sites were laid out in relation to astronomical alignments. In this lively book, Kehoe models for the general reader or undergraduate student how archaeologists tackle these and other controversies using empirical data, scientific method, and critical thinking. Drawing on examples from the archaeology of America's First Nations, the archaeology of religion, as well as debates over diffusion and independent invention and the capabilities of ancient technologies, Kehoe provides readers with the tools to think through controversies and arrive at sound assessments based on archaeological evidence.

Stephen W. Silliman, ed., *Engaging Archaeology: 25 Case Studies in Research Practice* (Oxford: Wiley Blackwell, 2018).

As all practicing archaeologists know, research seldom goes how we imagine it will when we embark on a new project. We start with questions and ideas (hunches, hypotheses) that shape our research design, but we often encounter hurdles, challenges, and evidence that flies in the face of what we think we know. In short, research is a messier process than described in final published reports. This edited collection of 25 case studies written by practicing archaeologists is equivalent to a back-stage pass to the process of archaeological research. Contributing authors reflect on how they conceptualized their projects, how they altered and revised their approaches in the face of on-the-ground circumstances, and how they worked with descendant communities and found new ways of communicating their research results. The collection describes projects that are both laboratory- and fieldwork-based, and includes examples of modest-sized projects similar to those that student readers of the collection might undertake.

Archaeology with Relevance to Contemporary Issues

William Balée, *Cultural Forests of the Amazon: A Historical Ecology of People and Their Landscapes* (Tuscaloosa: University of Alabama Press, 2013).

The Amazon basin is well recognized as a region of awesome biodiversity and forests that play a critical role in global climate dynamics. Although generations of scholars imagined the Amazon as a wilderness and its ecosystems a purely "natural" phenomenon, research over recent decades by archaeologists and environmental scientists has established the important role that Indigenous Amazonian peoples had in shaping the region's landscapes and biodiversity. Balée synthesizes a wealth of scholarship, including archaeological research, to lend new insight into the deep history of the Amazon basin. This rich historical ecology casts in new light the non-sustainable imported land-use strategies practiced today that have resulted in the biome's rapid destruction.

Anabel Ford and Ronald Nigh, *The Maya Forest Garden: Eight Millennia of Sustainable Cultivation of the*

Tropical Woodlands (Walnut Creek, CA: Left Coast Press, 2015).

One of the most pressing issues that confronts contemporary societies is sustainable food production. In this synthesis of what archaeology reveals about ancient Mayan agricultural practice, archaeologists Ford and Nigh describe how Mayan agriculture worked with the forested settings that it helped to create and sustain. These techniques have not been lost; they continue to inform small-scale Mayan agriculture today. The book is one of many examples that demonstrate the importance of place-based techniques and knowledge to sustainable food production and forest conservation.

Patricia A. McAnany and Norman Yoffee, eds., *Questioning Collapse: Human Resilience, Ecological Vulnerability and the Aftermath of Empire* (New York: Cambridge University Press, 2009).

This edited volume brings together archaeologists who have worked on the geographical case studies highlighted in the popular works of geographer Jared Diamond (e.g., his *Collapse: How Societies Choose to Fail or Succeed* [New York: Viking Penguin, 2005]). As telegraphed by the book's title, these authors challenge many of Diamond's key conclusions and explore how his focus on a progressivist framework in which cultures advance through complexity obscures how groups prove resilient in the face of challenge and change. The volume serves as an example of how close attention to archaeological evidence holds potential to improve public understanding of science.

Steven Mithen, with Sue Mithen, *Thirst: Water and Power in the Ancient World* (Cambridge, MA: Harvard University Press, 2012).

Archaeologists study a wide range of topics and questions relevant to present-day concerns. In this volume, Mithen explores practices of water management, hydraulic engineering, and the relationship between water and power (political and commercial) through archaeological case studies in the ancient Mediterranean world, China, Angkor, the American Southwest, together with Mayan and Incan civilizations. A final chapter reflects on implications of these archaeological examples for understanding challenges around managing water in contexts of climate change.

Michael Brian Schiffer, *Archaeology's Footprints in the Modern World* (Salt Lake City: University of Utah Press, 2017).

This book takes up the question of archaeology's value to present-day society. Using 42 case studies drawn from around the globe and a range of periods, Schiffer makes a case for how archaeology contributes to both scientific and humanist understandings of our shared human past and explores implications of archaeological findings for modern society. Written for a general audience, the book accessibly describes how archaeologists evaluate legends, complement historical understandings, enhance heritage awareness, collaborate with communities, contribute to social activism alongside the physical and biological sciences, and provide tools for environmental science, among other topics. In doing so, Schiffer argues that archaeology contributes as much to our understanding of the present as it does to that of the past.

Iconic Sites and Authoritative Summaries

Readers seeking authoritative summaries on the archaeology of particular areas of the world or topics will find a wealth of options through Oxford University Press's *Archaeology Handbooks*. The series includes dozens of titles that cover a wide range of geographical regions, periods, and topics (*https://www.oxfordhandbooks.com/page/50*).

Otherwise, here find some examples of authoritative summaries of iconic sites and the histories of their investigation:

Richard L. Burger and Lucy C. Salazar, eds., *Machu Picchu: Unveiling the Mystery of the Incas* (New Haven, CT: Yale University Press, 2008).

Originally prepared to accompany a museum exhibit of Incan artifacts, this illustrated volume authored by experts on the iconic Incan royal estate located high in the Peruvian cloud forest provides an authoritative overview of the site and recounts the history of investigations extending back to early 20th-century excavations by Yale archaeologist Hiram Bingham III.

Shadreck Chirikure, *Great Zimbabwe. Reclaiming a "Confiscated" Past* (London: Routledge, 2021).

An iconic monumental site in southern Africa, Great Zimbabwe has been subject to misinterpretation, reinterpretation, and now new interpretation in light of Indigenous African concepts and philosophies. Chirikure introduces readers to Shona concepts that lend new insight into life in this ancient urban settlement and its wider landscape. It is an example of how contemporary archaeology is enriched through local ways of knowing.

Alison E. Cooley, *Pompeii* (London: Duckworth, 2005).

Pompeii is a site synonymous with archaeology and among the world's iconic tourist destinations. Cooley's book combines a description of town life prior to Vesuvius' cataclysmic eruption in CE 79 with insights from research by volcanologists and archaeologists that help us to better understand the immediate effects and aftermath of the eruption. Though published some years ago, her account is consistent with a growing appreciation of archaeological sites as contemporary phenomena: existing in the present and their interpretation subject to the changing concerns of different times. Cooley describes the varying questions and concerns that motivated excavators of Pompeii site as it was "reawakened" during the 18th century, as it became a publicly accessible site valued for teaching youth about ancient Italian civilization in the 19th century, and as excavators became increasing interested in the town's deeper history in the 20th century. She demonstrates how each new question that is asked reveals new insights into Pompeii's rich and long history.

Mike Pitts, *How to Build Stonehenge* (New York: Thames & Hudson, 2022).

Readers looking for an account of how ancient people accomplished remarkable feats like quarrying and transport of large stones over substantial distances will find a readable account in Pitt's synthesis of recent research on Stonehenge. The book evaluates a range of explanations for how the stones were moved and raised, alongside vignettes about the history of investigations, curation of the monument, and folklore around the site.

Further Reading

Careers

A. Gwynn Henderson and Nicolas R. Laracuente, eds., "Special Forum: Careers in Archaeology," *The SAA Archaeological Record* 11, 2 (2011). (Available at *http://onlinedigeditions.com/publication/?i=65152*.)

This collection of short essays brings together practicing archaeologists working in the public and private (non-university) sectors who hold job titles ranging from city archaeologist, forensic investigator, tribal historic preservation officer, collections manager, non-profit fundraiser, and teacher, among others. The 12 contributors describe their career trajectories, talk about the challenges and benefits of their jobs, and provide advice for those who hope to pursue a similar career in archaeology.